NOTE

1. All recipes serve four unless otherwise stated.

2. All spoon measurements are level.

3. All eggs are sizes 3 or 4 unless otherwise stated.

4. Preparation times given are an average calculated during recipe testing.

5. Metric and imperial measurements have been calculated separately. Use one set of measurements only as they are not exact equivalents.

6. Cooking times may vary slightly depending on the individual oven. Dishes should be placed in the centre of the oven unless otherwise specified.

7. Always preheat the oven or grill to the specified temperature.

8. Spoon measures can be bought in both imperial and metric sizes to give accurate measurement of small quantities.

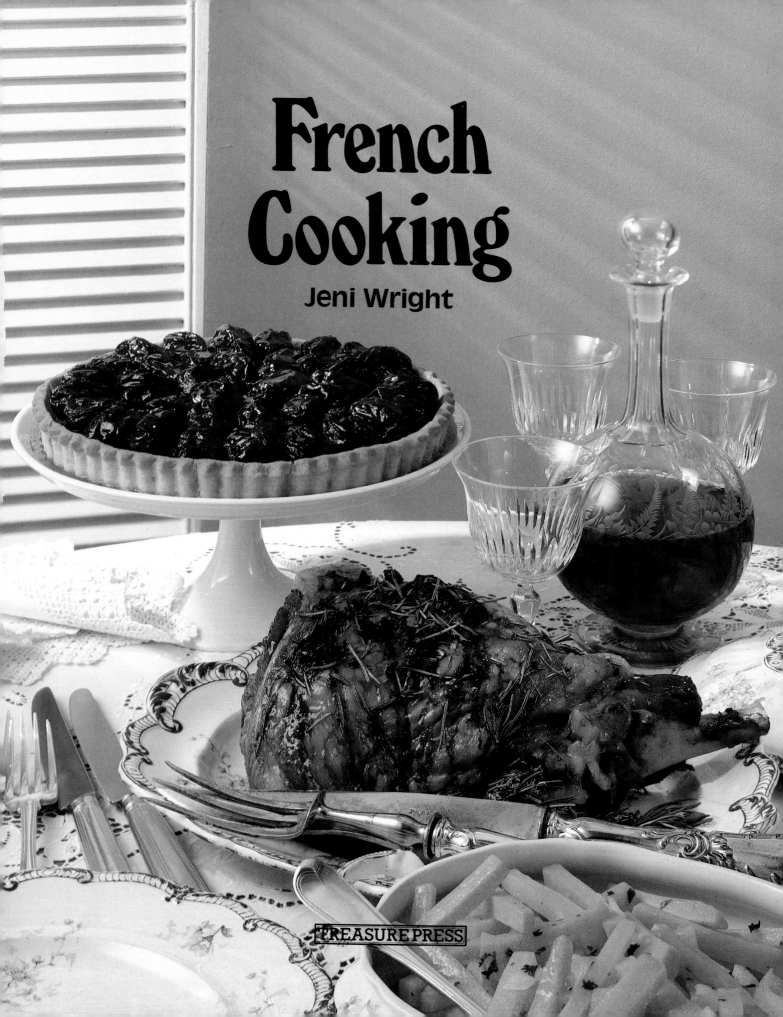

French Cooking

Jeni Wright

TREASURE PRESS

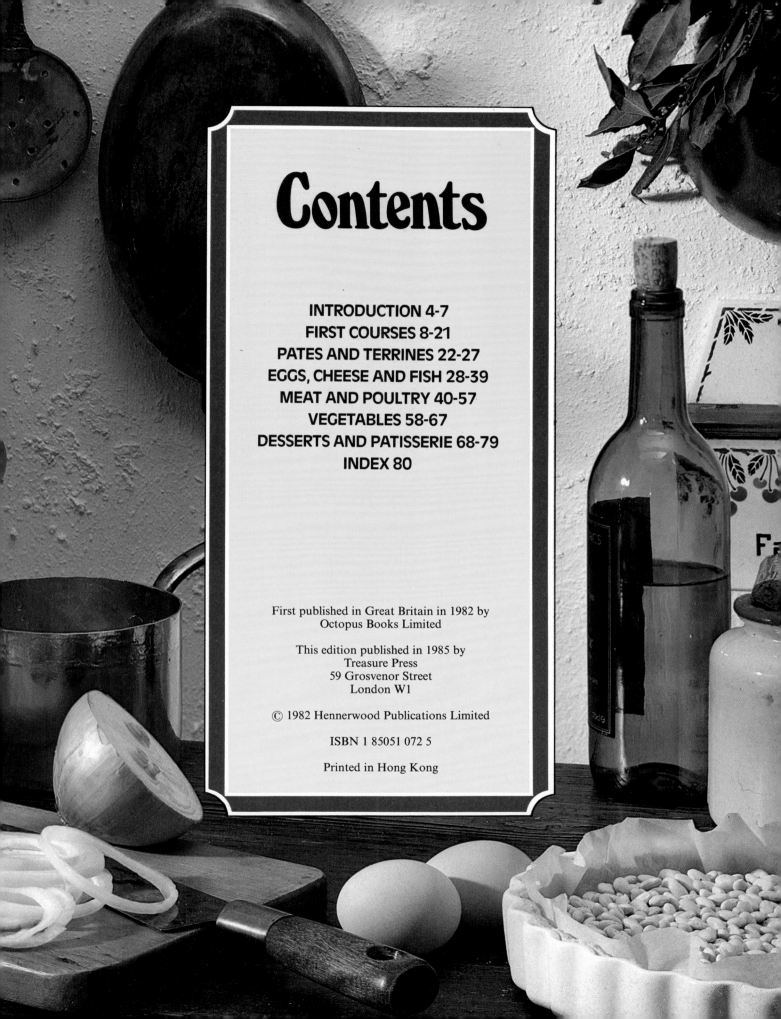

Contents

First published in Great Britain in 1982 by
Octopus Books Limited

This edition published in 1985 by
Treasure Press
59 Grosvenor Street
London W1

© 1982 Hennerwood Publications Limited

ISBN 1 85051 072 5

Printed in Hong Kong

INTRODUCTION

To the French, cooking is an art, and eating is one of the greatest pleasures in life. The high-class Parisian restaurant specializing in haute cuisine, the corner bistro with its regional specialities, the French housewife preparing a meal for her family, each has its or her own impeccably high standard of preparation and cooking, and each one cooks with the same care and attention.

To understand the French attitude to food, it is essential to start at the beginning with the raw ingredients, because to the French cook these are as important as the cooking itself. No amount of practise or skill can disguise inferior ingredients, and quality is always the order of the day. To shop in France is a joy in itself, not only to see the abundance of fresh produce, from the market stalls of brilliantly coloured vegetables and fruit to the impeccable displays of regional cheeses in the fromageries. Even though excellent modern supermarkets and hypermarkets cater for customers' tastes, most serious French cooks still prefer to go to the local market, charcuterie, poissonerie, etc., because in these specialist shops they can discuss their exact needs and the day's best purchases with the shopkeeper.

YOUR CHOICE OF INGREDIENTS

Shops and markets in Britain are obviously different from those in France, but if you are cooking French-style, do not be discouraged by the thought that you may not be able to buy the right ingredients here. French produce is imported into this country on a large scale, and most supermarkets stock the majority of items you will need. Delicatessens and delicatessen counters within supermarkets stock the more specialist items, and Continental greengrocers can be relied upon for high-quality imported vegetables. The ingredients for the recipes in this book can all be found in any good supermarket or delicatessen, butcher, fishmonger and greengrocer – and where an unusual ingredient might have been used in a similar French recipe, the recipe in this book has been adapted to suit the tastes and availability of ingredients in this country.

To help select the more unusual ingredients with which you may not be so familiar, the following checklist will be helpful.

Bacon Although bacon rashers are not used in France for frying and grilling as they are here, bacon is used to give flavour to many casseroles, stews and pâtés. Buy streaky bacon in the piece or thick belly pork rashers, and dice the meat or cut it into strips, depending on the dish. If available, salt pork gives added flavour, and is more similar in flavour to the French smoked belly of pork which is often used in preference to bacon, an expensive item in France.

Bouquet Garni A handy way to give a subtle flavour of herbs to casseroles, stews and soups, etc., a traditional bouquet garni (bunch of herbs) is made of sprigs of thyme and parsley and one or two bay leaves tied together with string. If fresh herbs are obtainable, then so much the better (many supermarkets sell these three fresh herbs packed together as a bouquet garni), but failing this, dried sachets are widely available. Look for the muslin bags which have string or ribbon attached, as these are the easiest to remove before serving.

Cheeses Many good French cheeses are exported to Britain, and with the advancements made in refrigerated transport their condition and quality is not dissimilar from their equivalents in France. Supermarkets sell the most popular varieties, which are most often imported pre-packaged straight from France. Whilst these are invariably of good quality, a Continental delicatessen will usually have a larger selection of cheeses for sale by the kilo/lb.

Brie, Camembert, and in particular Gruyère, are used often in this book. Brie and Camembert are unique French cheeses for which there are no substitutes, although since the two have a similar appearance and texture they are virtually inter-changeable in recipes – try them both and find which one you prefer. Gruyère in this country is usually imported from Switzerland rather than France, but this will make no difference to the recipes. If Emmental is more readily available, this can be used instead of Gruyère, but no other cheese will give quite the same melting qualities and distinctive flavour as these two, so it is inadvisable to use other alternatives. Goat's milk cheese, or chèvre, used for Tartelettes au Chèvre (page 19) is not so easy to obtain as other French cheeses, but can be found in some supermarkets and delicatessens with good cheese counters. This type of cheese is usually tangier in flavour than cow's milk cheese, and some varieties are very salty.

The French love of cheese far exceeds that of any other country in the world. Cheese is almost always served at every French meal, after the main course. French bread (without butter) may be broken into small pieces and eaten with the cheese, but it is often eaten on its own with any remaining wine and perhaps a few grapes as accompaniments. The French cheeseboard is rarely elaborate, and for most family meals there will be only one, or at the most two, cheeses served – at exactly the right degree of ripeness. In general, desserts are not so popular as they are here (except perhaps with children who often eat yogurt for dessert or a soft white cheese topped with fruit and sugar), and so the cheese marks the end of the meal.

Cream In France there is no equivalent to our single or double cream, and cream is seldom served with puddings and desserts. Fresh cream (crème fraîche) in France has an altogether sharper or tarter flavour than our creams and is more often used in cooking, both in sweet and savoury dishes. Many of the recipes in this book use cream as a thickening agent just before serving – this is a favourite French method of enriching and thickening sauces, particularly if they are to be served with meat, poultry and fish. Crème fraîche is ideal for this because it is not sweet; it also reduces and thickens sauces beautifully without curdling. Because it is not available in this country, the recipes in this book specify double cream wherever crème fraîche might have been used in France. However greater care must be taken with double cream because it has a lower fat content than crème fraîche, and is more likely to separate and become oily. When adding it to a sauce or other liquid, use a heavy-based pan (cast iron is best) and whisk it in with a wire balloon whisk. Bring slowly to the boil and simmer until the liquid reduces and thickens, whisking vigorously all the time. The amount of time this will take varies according to the pan used and the amount of liquid and cream, but it can take as long as 15 minutes. The important thing to remember is to stand over it all the time and to whisk constantly. Double cream will never have quite the body and piquancy of crème fraîche, but used carefully it is a perfectly acceptable substitute.

Garlic To many people in this country, the word garlic is synonymous with French cooking! Garlic is used all over France (especially in the south along the Mediterranean coast and towards the Spanish and Italian borders). Although the French do love garlic, it is not necessary for it to be included in every dish to give it a 'French' flavour. When garlic is used in the recipes in this book, the quantities given are intended only as a guide, and you can use as much or as little as you like. In summer and early autumn look for the purple-skinned varieties imported from France as these tend to be milder.

If you are unused to the flavour of garlic, treat it with caution at first until you and your family have grown accustomed to it. A bulb of garlic is made up of several individual sections or cloves. To separate them, place the bulb on a board or work surface and bang it firmly with the heel of your hand. Peel individual cloves with your fingers, then cut into small pieces with a sharp knife. Put about 2.5 ml/½ teaspoon salt on the board and, working with the flat of the blade of a large cook's knife, crush the garlic and salt to a paste. If you crush garlic in this way,

it becomes absorbed much easier and is therefore more digestible. For a more subtle flavour of garlic, simply cut a clove in half and rub the cut surface around the inside of cooking pans and salad bowls, etc. Or 'bruise' a clove of garlic by flattening it with a pestle or blade of a knife, then add it to a sauce, soup or casserole and remove it before serving. A tip for avoiding 'garlic breath' is to chew a sprig or two of fresh parsley!

Herbs Used extensively, fresh herbs are always preferred to dried and are more readily available in France than they are here. Chervil, chives, parsley, rosemary, savory and tarragon are commonly used in French dishes, and all are relatively easy to grow in a sunny sheltered spot in the garden. Tie sprigs together and add to liquids as for a bouquet garni, or chop finely and sprinkle into dishes before cooking; chopped herbs are also often sprinkled over savoury dishes as a garnish. Bay leaves are frequently added to casseroles, sauces and soups to give a subtle flavour, but remember always to remove before serving. Wherever possible in the recipes in this book, try to use fresh herbs; dried can be used as a substitute, but they are more pungent and only half the quantity given for fresh should be used. Dried herbs do not keep their aroma and flavour for long (about 3 months), so it is best to buy them in small quantities and check before use – stale dried herbs can impart a bitter, even musty flavour to a dish.

Mustard The French are great mustard lovers, and there are many different French mustards imported into this country. Although British mustard manu-

facturers make jars of 'French mustard' in paste form, it is preferable to use one of the more specific French mustards. French mustards are not sold in powder form like some English mustards, but they are very convenient to use in cooking to add piquancy and sharpness to sauces and casseroles, etc. Many different varieties of Dijon mustard are sold in Britain; sharp rather than hot, they are always smooth-textured and vary in colour from pale yellow ochre through to greeny yellow (this type is made from green peppercorns), and light muddy brown. The pale-coloured varieties are most suitable for cooking, especially in sauces. Another popular French mustard is Moutarde de Meaux, a whole-grain type which tends to be milder in flavour than Dijon, but the granular texture is not always suitable for dishes with smooth sauces. When adding any mustard during cooking, never let it boil or it will impart an overriding bitterness to the finished dish. The best way to avoid this is to stir in the mustard off the heat, just before serving.

Oil For frying, the French tend to use oil in preference to butter and other fats (except perhaps in Normandy and neighbouring northern regions where locally churned butter is popular). Light vegetable oils with little flavour are preferred for most dishes, and any corn, safflower, sunflower or soya bean oil can be used. For salads, mayonnaise and salad dressings, however, olive oil is the one to choose, and the fruitier and greener it is the better. Provençal olive oil is considered one of the best – in Provence it adds its unique fruity flavour to all cooked dishes as well as salads. Olive oil is expensive in Britain, but there is

no substitute for its thick consistency and flavour. Buy the best quality you can afford or your salads and dressings may be disappointingly flavourless. Although it is very expensive, the distinctive nutty flavour of walnut oil is becoming increasingly popular in France for salad dressings.

Shallots When glancing through any French cookery book it seems that almost all savoury dishes start by frying shallots, in oil. One of the mildest members of the onion family, the shallot is not so widely used here in Britain as it is in France. If you do not grow your own, look for them in spring and summer at specialist greengrocers and markets, because their mild flavour is more suited to French dishes than other pungent onions. Wherever shallots are used in a recipe and you find them difficult to obtain, use spring onions or half the quantity of mild Spanish onions instead.

Successful Pastry

The French method of making pastry is slightly different from our own in that a higher proportion of fat to flour is used, resulting in a richer, shorter and crisper finish. Pâte brisée is the closest French equivalent to our shortcrust pastry. Sweet shortcrust pastry (pâte sucrée) for flans and tarts, has sugar added during the making of the dough, before cutting in the butter, and for an even richer pastry known as pâte sablée or French flan pastry, one or more egg yolks are added.

The high fat content of these pastries makes them more difficult to handle than other less rich mixtures, therefore extra care should be taken when making them. Always work in the coolest possible temperature and make sure that your work surface and utensils are cold (marble is the best work surface for pastry-making). Warm hands can ruin the rubbing-in process, so before starting to make pastry, hold your hands under cold running water to ensure they keep cool, then dry them quickly. Work quickly and lightly, using only your fingertips and lifting the mixture high above the bowl to aerate it. After rubbing-in, form the dough into a ball with one hand only, taking great care not to overwork the mixture or it will become oily – simply gather it together loosely without pressing and kneading. Once formed into a ball, cover with cling film or foil and chill in the refrigerator for at least 30 minutes to let the dough cool and relax.

To roll out rich doughs, place the ball on a lightly floured surface and flatten with a floured rolling pin. Shape by rolling in short sharp strokes, working from the centre outwards, taking care not to press down too hard. Turn the shape round frequently as you roll, but do not turn the dough over. Transfer to the flan tin or ring by carefully lifting on to the rolling pin, then ease into the tin with the fingertips, making sure you do not stretch the dough. (If the dough is too sticky to handle it is often easier not to roll it out at all, but simply to place the ball of dough in the tin or ring and press it gently into shape with the fingertips.) Patch any cracks with trimmings, pressing them neatly to seal. To help prevent rich doughs shrinking chill again for about 30 minutes before baking.

FIRST COURSES

Invariably simple, at least for family meals, the French serve delicious first courses to whet the appetite in preparation for what is to follow. A simple salad, one or two cooked vegetables tossed in a well seasoned dressing, maybe a slice or two of pâté, ham, salami or other cooked meat from the local charcuterie, a fillet of smoked fish – these are the kinds of things you might be offered in a French home. The first courses and soups in this chapter are more likely to be served at dinner parties or on other special occasions, but many will serve as light supper dishes for fewer people, and the hearty type of soups are often eaten as meals in themselves, with chunks of fresh French bread.

Salade parisienne
Parisian salad

Metric	*Imperial*
100 g button mushrooms, halved or sliced if large	*4 oz button mushrooms, halved or sliced if large*
175 g piece garlic sausage, diced	*6 oz piece garlic sausage, diced*
100 g Saint Paulin or Tomme de Savoie cheese, rind removed, diced	*4 oz Saint Paulin or Tomme de Savoie cheese, rind removed, diced*
50 g shelled walnut halves (optional)	*2 oz shelled walnut halves (optional)*
1 lettuce, separated into leaves	*1 lettuce, separated into leaves*

Dressing:	*Dressing:*
6 × 15 ml spoons walnut oil	*6 tablespoons walnut oil*
2 × 15 ml spoons cider vinegar	*2 tablespoons cider vinegar*
2 × 5 ml spoons light Dijon mustard	*2 teaspoons light Dijon mustard*
salt	*salt*
freshly ground black pepper	*freshly ground black pepper*

Preparation time: 10 minutes

Walnut oil is available in bottles from good delicatessens. Alternatively, make your own by crushing 50 g/2 oz shelled walnuts in a mortar and pestle, or with a rolling pin, and adding 120 ml/4 fl oz olive oil.

Put all the ingredients for the dressing in a screw-topped jar, and shake well to mix.
Put the mushrooms, garlic sausage, cheese and walnuts in a bowl, pour over the dressing and toss gently. Arrange the lettuce leaves around the bottom and sides of a salad bowl. Spoon the salad mixture in the centre and serve immediately.

Salade parisienne; Tomates farcies aux crevettes

Tomates farcies aux crevettes
Tomatoes stuffed with prawns

Metric
8 medium tomatoes
salt
225 g peeled prawns,
    defrosted if frozen
2 hard-boiled eggs, finely
    chopped
2 × 15 ml spoons finely
    chopped parsley
finely grated rind of 1
    lemon
freshly ground black
    pepper
8 unpeeled prawns, to
    garnish (optional)

**Aïoli (garlic
mayonnaise):**
2 large garlic cloves,
    peeled
1 × 1.25 ml spoon light
    Dijon or other French
    mustard
1 egg yolk
300 ml olive oil

Imperial
8 medium tomatoes
salt
8 oz peeled prawns,
    defrosted if frozen
2 hard-boiled eggs, finely
    chopped
2 tablespoons finely
    chopped parsley
finely grated rind of 1
    lemon
freshly ground black
    pepper
8 unpeeled prawns, to
    garnish (optional)

**Aïoli (garlic
mayonnaise):**
2 large garlic cloves,
    peeled
¼ teaspoon light Dijon or
    other French
    mustard
1 egg yolk
½ pint olive oil

Preparation time: 25–30 minutes

In France, a mortar and pestle are commonly used when making mayonnaise. An electric blender or food processor can be used, following the same instructions given here, but using 1 whole egg in addition to the egg yolk.

Cut the tops (stalk ends) off the tomatoes and reserve. Scoop out all the flesh and seeds from the insides of the tomatoes with a teaspoon, taking care not to break the shells. Sprinkle a little salt inside the tomatoes, then stand them upside down on a board and leave for 10–15 minutes to drain.
Meanwhile, make the aïoli. Put the garlic cloves in a mortar with 1 × 2.5 ml spoon/½ teaspoon salt. Crush the garlic and salt with a pestle, then work in the mustard and egg yolk. Add the olive oil a drop at a time until the mixture begins to thicken, then add the oil in a thin, steady stream until all is incorporated and the aïoli is very thick, working constantly with the pestle to amalgamate the egg yolk and oil. Set on one side.
Dry the prawns thoroughly with paper towels, then chop roughly. Fold into the aïoli with the chopped eggs, parsley and lemon rind. Add salt and pepper to taste.
Stand the tomatoes upright on a serving plate. Spoon the prawn mixture into them and place the reserved tops on the slant. Garnish each tomato with an unpeeled prawn, if using. Serve at room temperature.

Saumon fumé à la mousse de fromage
Stuffed smoked salmon rolls

Metric	Imperial
1 envelope (15 g) powdered gelatine	1 envelope (½ oz) powdered gelatine
3 × 15 ml spoons lemon juice	3 tablespoons lemon juice
1 × 15 ml spoon water	1 tablespoon water
225 g full-fat soft cheese	8 oz full-fat soft cheese
1 bunch spring onions, trimmed and finely chopped	1 bunch spring onions, trimmed and finely chopped
2 × 15 ml spoons chopped chives	2 tablespoons chopped chives
4 × 15 ml spoons thick mayonnaise or double cream, lightly whipped	4 tablespoons thick mayonnaise or double cream, lightly whipped
salt	salt
freshly ground black pepper	freshly ground black pepper
8 thin slices smoked salmon (total weight about 225 g)	8 thin slices smoked salmon (total weight about 8 oz)
2 lemons, cut into wedges, to serve	2 lemons, cut into wedges, to serve

Preparation time: 30 minutes, plus chilling

Sprinkle the gelatine over the lemon juice and water in a heatproof bowl. Leave until spongy, then place the bowl in a pan of gently simmering water. Heat gently until the gelatine has dissolved, stirring occasionally. Leave to cool slightly.

Meanwhile, put the cheese in a bowl and beat with a wooden spoon until soft. Beat in the spring onions and chives, then the mayonnaise or double cream and salt and pepper to taste.

Fold in the gelatine liquid until evenly blended, then cover and chill in the refrigerator until the mixture is firm, but not set.

Lay the salmon slices flat on a board or work surface. Divide the cheese mixture equally between them, placing it at one end of each slice, then rolling the salmon up around the filling as neatly as possible.

Place the salmon rolls on a serving platter and chill in the refrigerator for at least 4 hours, preferably overnight. Before serving, sprinkle with pepper and garnish with lemon wedges. Serve chilled.

Crème Du Barry
Cream of cauliflower soup

Metric	Imperial
40 g butter	1½ oz butter
1 onion, peeled and finely chopped	1 onion, peeled and finely chopped
1 × 450 g cauliflower, divided into florets	1 × 1 lb cauliflower, divided into florets
600 ml chicken stock	1 pint chicken stock
2 × 5 ml spoons freshly chopped chervil or 1 × 5 ml spoon dried chervil	2 teaspoons freshly chopped chervil or 1 teaspoon dried chervil
salt	salt
freshly ground black pepper	freshly ground black pepper
600 ml milk	1 pint milk

Preparation time: 15 minutes, plus cooling
Cooking time: about 40 minutes

This is a simpler version of the classic French soup of the same name.

Melt 25 g/1 oz butter in a heavy-based pan, add the onion and fry gently until soft. Add the cauliflower florets, reserving a few tiny sprigs for the garnish. Cook the cauliflower over gentle heat for about 5 minutes, stirring all the time until coated in the butter and onion.

Stir in the stock and bring to the boil. Lower the heat, add half the chervil, and salt and pepper to taste, then half cover with a lid. Simmer gently for 20 minutes until the cauliflower is tender, stirring occasionally.

Remove from the heat and leave to cool slightly, then purée in an electric blender or work through a sieve until smooth.

Return the purée to the rinsed-out pan and stir in the milk. Bring to just below boiling point, stirring constantly, then simmer gently for about 5 minutes. Check the consistency of the soup, stirring in a little extra milk if it seems too thick.

Meanwhile, melt the remaining butter in a separate pan, add the reserved cauliflower sprigs and toss gently in the butter for 1–2 minutes.

Taste and adjust the seasoning of the soup, then pour into a warmed tureen or 4 individual bowls. Place a few cauliflower sprigs in each serving, then sprinkle with the remaining chervil. Alternatively, leave a few pieces of chervil whole for garnishing. Serve immediately.

Saumon fumé à la mousse de fromage; Crème Du Barry; Crème de courgettes au brie

Crème de courgettes au brie
Courgette and Brie cream soup

Metric	*Imperial*
350 g courgettes, sliced	*12 oz courgettes, sliced*
3 small potatoes, peeled and quartered	*3 small potatoes, peeled and quartered*
1 × 15 ml spoon olive oil	*1 tablespoon olive oil*
salt	*salt*
100 g soft ripe Brie cheese, rind removed, diced	*4 oz soft ripe Brie cheese, rind removed, diced*
freshly ground white pepper	*freshly ground white pepper*
4 × 15 ml spoons double cream	*4 tablespoons double cream*

Preparation time: 15 minutes, plus cooling
Cooking time: about 30 minutes

Put the courgettes in a large pan with the potatoes, oil and 1 × 5 ml spoon/1 teaspoon salt. Cover with water and stir well. Bring to the boil, then lower the heat and simmer for 15–20 minutes until the potatoes are tender. Leave to cool slightly.
Remove the courgettes and potatoes with a slotted spoon and place in an electric blender. Add the diced Brie and 300 ml/½ pint of the cooking liquid from the vegetables. Blend until smooth.
Return the mixture to the rinsed-out pan and add a further 150 ml/¼ pint cooking liquid from the vegetables. Bring to just below boiling point, stirring all the time, then add salt and pepper to taste. Check the consistency of the soup and add more vegetable liquid or water if it is too thick.
Pour into 4 warmed individual bowls and swirl a spoonful of cream into each. Serve immediately with French bread.

Champignons Kiev
Fried mushrooms with garlic butter

Metric
24 cup mushrooms
100 g unsalted butter,
  softened
2–3 garlic cloves, peeled
  and crushed with
  1 × 2.5 ml spoon salt
2 × 15 ml spoons finely
  chopped parsley
freshly ground black
  pepper
2 eggs
75 dried breadcrumbs
vegetable oil for deep-
  frying

Imperial
24 cup mushrooms
4 oz unsalted butter,
  softened
2–3 garlic cloves, peeled
  and crushed with
  ½ teaspoon salt
2 tablespoons finely
  chopped parsley
freshly ground black
  pepper
2 eggs
3 oz dried breadcrumbs
vegetable oil for deep-
  frying

Preparation time: about 1 hour, plus chilling
Cooking time: about 20 minutes

It is important to use deep, cup-shaped mushrooms so that they will contain the garlic butter. Cup mushrooms are the medium-sized cultivated mushrooms as opposed to the small button or large open (flat) mushrooms.

Wipe the mushrooms clean with a damp cloth, but do not wash or peel them. Carefully pull out the stalks, keeping the caps whole. Dry the caps with paper towels. Chop the stalks very finely.

Put the softened butter in a bowl with the chopped mushroom stalks, garlic, parsley and pepper to taste. Beat together well. Spoon into the mushroom cavities, then sandwich the mushrooms together in pairs. Use cocktail sticks to secure them.

Beat the eggs lightly in a bowl and spread the breadcrumbs out on a plate. Dip the mushroom pairs one at a time into the beaten egg, then roll them in the breadcrumbs. Repeat this process once more until the mushrooms are evenly and thoroughly coated. Chill in the refrigerator for at least 1 hour.

Heat the oil in a deep-fat fryer to 190°C/375°F, or until a stale bread cube turns golden in 40–50 seconds. Fry the mushrooms a few at a time for about 5 minutes, turning them frequently with a slotted spoon until golden brown and crisp on all sides. Drain on paper towels and keep hot while frying the remainder. Remove the cocktail sticks and serve immediately.

Champignons Kiev; Salade de riz provençale

Salade de riz provençale
Provencal rice salad

Metric	Imperial
450 g fresh mussels, scrubbed, with beards removed	1 lb fresh mussels, scrubbed, with beards removed
225 g long-grain rice	8 oz long-grain rice
900 ml water	1½ pints water
pinch of saffron powder (optional)	pinch of saffron powder (optional)
salt	salt
2 shallots or 1 small onion, peeled and finely chopped	2 shallots or 1 small onion, peeled and finely chopped
½ red pepper, cored, seeded and finely chopped	½ red pepper, cored, seeded and finely chopped
½ green paper, cored, seeded and finely chopped	½ green pepper, cored, seeded and finely chopped
3 tomatoes, skinned, seeded and chopped	3 tomatoes, skinned, seeded and chopped
50 g black olives, halved, pitted and chopped	2 oz black olives, halved, pitted and chopped

Dressing:

Dressing:	Dressing:
2 garlic cloves, peeled and crushed with 1 × 2.5 ml spoon salt	2 garlic cloves, peeled and crushed with ½ teaspoon salt
1 egg yolk	1 egg yolk
6 × 15 ml spoons olive oil	6 tablespoons olive oil
2 × 15 ml spoons wine vinegar	2 tablespoons wine vinegar
2 × 15 ml spoons Pernod (optional)	2 tablespoons Pernod (optional)
2 × 15 ml spoons freshly chopped parsley	2 tablespoons freshly chopped parsley
freshly ground black pepper	freshly ground black pepper

Preparation time: about 45 minutes, plus soaking
Cooking time: 35–40 minutes

To save time, and when fresh mussels are not available, use frozen mussels. These are sold on the half shell by freezer centres and large supermarkets, and are precooked. Simply defrost them according to the package instructions and fold them straight into the salad.

Soak the fresh mussels in cold water for about 1 hour. Put the rice in a large pan with the water, saffron and a pinch of salt. Bring to the boil, stir once, then cover with a tight-fitting lid and lower the heat. Simmer gently for 15–20 minutes, until the rice is tender yet firm to the bite.
Meanwhile, drain the mussels and discard any which are open. Place the closed mussels in a large saucepan with a little water. Bring to the boil, cover and simmer for 10 minutes, shaking the pan frequently. Drain, and discard any unopened mussels. Remove the mussels from their shells, reserving a few in their shells for the garnish.
Drain the cooked rice and make the dressing. Put the garlic and egg yolk in a bowl and whisk with a fork. Whisk in the oil gradually, then the wine vinegar and Pernod, if using. Add the chopped parsley, and salt and pepper to taste.
Turn the warm rice into a large salad bowl and pour in the dressing. Fork the dressing evenly through the rice, then leave until cold.
Add the vegetables and olives to the rice and fork in gently. Fold in the shelled mussels, slicing them in halves or quarters if they are large. Taste and adjust the seasoning. Serve at room temperature, garnished with the reserved mussels left in their shells.

Variation:
Instead of mussels, use 1 × 200 g/7 oz can tuna, drained and flaked, and 1 × 50 g/2 oz can anchovies, drained, soaked in milk for 20 minutes, then drained and chopped.

Garbure
Bean and cabbage soup

Metric	Imperial
225 g dried haricot beans, soaked in cold water overnight	8 oz dried haricot beans, soaked in cold water overnight
450 g belly pork rashers	1 lb belly pork rashers
1 small ham knuckle	1 small ham knuckle
1 bouquet garni	1 bouquet garni
3 carrots, peeled and thickly sliced	3 carrots, peeled and thickly sliced
2 leeks, thickly sliced	2 leeks, thickly sliced
2 turnips, peeled and thickly sliced	2 turnips, peeled and thickly sliced
1 onion, peeled and sliced	1 onion, peeled and sliced
3 garlic cloves, peeled	3 garlic cloves, peeled
1 × 1.25 ml spoon cayenne pepper	¼ teaspoon cayenne pepper
salt	salt
450 g firm cabbage, sliced	1 lb firm cabbage, sliced
freshly chopped parsley, to garnish	freshly chopped parsley, to garnish

Preparation time: about 30 minutes, plus soaking
Cooking time: 1¾ hours

Garbure is a main course soup, popular in country districts. You may use salt pork if preferred (in which case it should be soaked in cold water overnight). The vegetables used can be varied according to the time of year—in summer, for example, fresh French beans may be substituted for the dried haricot beans. Potatoes can be included for a thicker consistency.

Drain the beans and place in a large pan with the pork, ham knuckle and bouquet garni. Cover with fresh cold water and bring to the boil, skimming off any scum. Lower the heat, half cover with a lid and simmer for 30 minutes.
Add the vegetables (except the cabbage), the garlic, cayenne, and salt to taste, then add enough cold water to cover all the ingredients. Bring to the boil, then lower the heat, half cover and simmer for 1 hour until all the meat and vegetables are very soft. Stir in the cabbage and continue cooking a further 15 minutes.
Remove the pork and ham from the soup, then cut the meat into small pieces, discarding all bones and rinds. Discard the bouquet garni, then return the meat to the pan and heat through, adding more water if the soup is too thick. Taste and adjust the seasoning, then serve hot, sprinkled with parsley.
Serves 4–6

Soupe à la bière
Beer soup

Metric	Imperial
25 g butter	1 oz butter
1 × 15 ml spoon olive oil	1 tablespoon olive oil
2 large onions, peeled and finely sliced	2 large onions, peeled and finely sliced
pinch of soft brown sugar	pinch of soft brown sugar
75 g fresh white breadcrumbs	3 oz fresh white breadcrumbs
600 ml light ale	1 pint light ale
600 ml chicken stock or water	1 pint chicken stock or water
salt	salt
freshly ground black pepper	freshly ground black pepper

To finish:

Metric	Imperial
4 slices French bread	4 slices French bread
4 × 5 ml spoons brandy (optional)	4 teaspoons brandy (optional)
about 50 g Gruyère or Parmesan cheese, finely grated	about 2 oz Gruyère or Parmesan cheese, finely grated

Preparation time: about 25 minutes, plus cooling
Cooking time: about 55 minutes

In the northern regions of France bordering on Belgium, beer is as popular a drink as wine is in other parts of France. Since French beers are not available in Britain, a light ale is our nearest equivalent.
Use the Parmesan cheese for a sharper flavour.

Melt the butter with the oil in a heavy-based pan, add the onions. Cover and cook gently for 15 minutes, stirring and checking that they do not burn.
When the onions are soft and lightly coloured, sprinkle in the sugar. Stir for 1–2 minutes, then add the breadcrumbs. Stir again for a few minutes until lightly coloured, then stir in the light ale and chicken stock or water with salt and pepper to taste.
Bring to the boil, then lower the heat, half cover the pan and simmer gently for 30 minutes, stirring occasionally. Leave to cool slightly.
Purée the soup in an electric blender or work in a mouli-legumes (vegetable mill) until smooth. Return the purée to the rinsed out pan and bring to just below boiling point, stirring constantly. Simmer gently for about 5 minutes, then check the consistency, stirring in a little water if it seems too thick.
To finish, place 1 slice of bread in each of 4 warmed individual bowls. Pour the soup into the bowls, then sprinkle 1 × 5 ml spoon/1 teaspoon brandy into each serving, if using. Serve immediately, with the grated cheese handed separately.

Goujons de sole au fromage
Deep-fried sole with cheese

Metric

2 Dover or lemon sole,
    divided into 8 fillets,
    skinned
75–100 g Gruyère cheese
about 2 × 15 ml spoons
    plain flour, for coating
2 eggs, beaten
100–175 g white
    breadcrumbs
salt
freshly ground black
    pepper
vegetable oil, for deep-
    frying

To serve:
lemon wedges
tartare sauce

Imperial

2 Dover or lemon sole,
    divided into 8 fillets,
    skinned
3–4 oz Gruyère cheese
about 2 tablespoons plain
    flour, for coating
2 eggs, beaten
4–6 oz white
    breadcrumbs
salt
freshly ground black
    pepper
vegetable oil, for deep-
    frying

To serve:
lemon wedges
tartare sauce

Garbure; Soupe à la bière; Goujons de sole au fromage

Preparation time: about 45 minutes, plus chilling
Cooking time: 15–20 minutes

Make the breadcrumbs from bread that is stale (at least 2 days old) or they will not adhere to the egg. If sole is unavailable use plaice instead.

Cut each sole fillet horizontally in half to make 16 strips of fish. Sprinkle with salt and pepper. Cut the cheese into strips or cubes the same width as the fish. Place 1 strip of cheese at one end of a strip of fish, then roll the fish up round the cheese. Secure with 1 or 2 wooden cocktail sticks. Repeat with the remaining fish and cheese.
Coat the fish parcels lightly in flour. Put the beaten eggs in a wide, shallow bowl. Spread the breadcrumbs out on a plate. Dip the fish in the egg, then in the breadcrumbs until evenly coated. Repeat these layers once more to ensure that the fish and cheese are completely covered, pressing the coating on firmly to adhere. Chill in the refrigerator for at least 30 minutes.
Heat the oil in a deep-fat frier to 190°C/375°F or until a stale bread cube turns golden in 40–50 seconds. Deep-fry the goujons in batches for 3–5 minutes until golden brown and crisp, turning them over during frying. Drain on paper towels and keep hot while frying the remainder. Serve at once, with lemon wedges and tartare sauce.

Pâtes d'anchois
Anchovy pastries

Metric
1 × 50 g can anchovies, drained and soaked in milk for 20 minutes
2 hard-boiled eggs, very finely chopped
2 tomatoes, skinned, seeded and very finely chopped
2 × 15 ml spoons very finely chopped parsley
2 × 5 ml spoons tomato purée
1 × 2.5 ml spoon anchovy essence (optional)
freshly ground black pepper
1 × 400 g packet frozen puff pastry, defrosted
1 small egg, beaten, to glaze
cayenne pepper

Imperial
1 × 2 oz can anchovies, drained and soaked in milk for 20 minutes
2 hard-boiled eggs, very finely chopped
2 tomatoes, skinned, seeded and very finely chopped
2 tablespoons very finely chopped parsley
2 teaspoons tomato purée
½ teaspoon anchovy essence (optional)
freshly ground black pepper
1 × 14 oz packet frozen puff pastry, defrosted
1 small egg, beaten, to glaze
cayenne pepper

Preparation time: about 50 minutes, plus soaking
Cooking time: 15 minutes
Oven: 200°C, 400°F, Gas Mark 6

Drain the anchovies, pat dry with paper towels, then chop roughly. Put the anchovies in a bowl with the chopped eggs, tomatoes and parsley, the tomato purée, anchovy essence, and pepper to taste. Mix thoroughly, then set aside.

Roll out half the pastry thinly on a floured surface, then cut into 14–16 'fish' shapes, each one about 10 cm/4 inches long and about 4 cm/1½ inches at the widest point. (If you find it helpful use a paper pattern.) Spread a spoonful of the anchovy mixture on each piece of pastry, piling it up in the centre and leaving a narrow margin around the edge. Place the shapes on dampened baking sheets and brush the exposed edges of the pastry with water.

Roll out the remaining pastry and cut into the similar shapes, but a little larger, to make lids. Place over the anchovy filling and press the edges down firmly to seal. Brush with beaten egg, then make 3 slashes in the top of each pastry and sprinkle with a little cayenne.

Bake the pastries in a preheated oven for 15 minutes or until they are puffed up and golden brown. Transfer carefully with a spatula to a wire rack to cool for 5 minutes. Serve warm.
Makes 14–16

Chaussons
Spinach and cheese puffs

Metric
100 g frozen chopped spinach, defrosted
1 × 400 g packet frozen puff pastry, defrosted
100 g full-fat soft cheese flavoured with garlic and herbs
freshly ground black pepper
vegetable oil, for deep-frying
1 egg, beaten, to glaze

Imperial
4 oz frozen chopped spinach, defrosted
1 × 14 oz packet frozen puff pastry, defrosted
4 oz full-fat soft cheese flavoured with garlic and herbs
freshly ground black pepper
vegetable oil, for deep-frying
1 egg, beaten, to glaze

Preparation time: about 30 minutes
Cooking time: about 25 minutes

Put the spinach in a heavy-based pan and cook over a low heat until completely dry, stirring frequently. Leave to cool.

Meanwhile, roll out the pastry thinly on a floured surface and cut into about 20 × 7.5 cm/3 inch circles. Beat the cheese in a bowl until soft, then beat in the spinach and pepper to taste. Put about 1 × 5 ml spoon/1 teaspoon spinach and cheese filling in the centre of each pastry circle and fold the pastry over. Pinch the edges together at the top to seal.

Heat the oil in a deep-fat fryer to 190°C/375°F or until a stale bread cube turns golden in 40–50 seconds. Dip the chaussons in the beaten egg until evenly coated, then deep-fry a few at a time for 3–4 minutes until puffed up and golden. Remove with a slotted spoon and drain on paper towels. Keep hot while frying the remainder. Serve at once, using cocktail sticks, if preferred.
Makes about 20

Moules farcies à la crème
Stuffed mussels baked with cream

Preparation time: about 45 minutes, plus soaking
Cooking time: 55 minutes
Oven: 190°C, 375°F, Gas Mark 5

Metric	Imperial
48 mussels, scrubbed, and beards removed	*48 mussels, scrubbed, and beards removed*
150 ml dry white wine	*¼ pint dry white wine*
150 ml water	*¼ pint water*
1 bouquet garni	*1 bouquet garni*
100 g unsalted butter	*4 oz unsalted butter*
2 shallots or 1 small onion, peeled and very finely chopped	*2 shallots or 1 small onion, peeled and very finely chopped*
1–2 garlic cloves, peeled and crushed with 1 × 2.5 ml spoon salt	*1–2 garlic cloves, peeled and crushed with ½ teaspoon salt*
175 g button mushrooms, very finely chopped	*6 oz button mushrooms, very finely chopped*
2 × 15 ml spoons freshly chopped parsley	*2 tablespoons freshly chopped parsley*
75 g fresh white bread-crumbs	*3 oz fresh white bread-crumbs*
150 ml double cream	*¼ pint double cream*
freshly ground black pepper	*freshly ground black pepper*
about 2 × 15 ml spoons grated Parmesan cheese (optional)	*about 2 tablespoons grated Parmesan cheese (optional)*

This is an ideal dish for using frozen mussels on the half shell. Simply defrost, chop and stuff them, then bake in a sauce made from half white wine and half fish or chicken stock.

Soak the mussels in cold water for about 1 hour. Drain the mussels and discard any which are open. Place the closed mussels in a large saucepan with the wine, water and bouquet garni. Bring to the boil, cover with a tight-fitting lid and simmer for 10 minutes, shaking the pan frequently during this time. Meanwhile, melt 25 g/1 oz butter in a pan, add the shallots, or onion, and garlic and fry gently until soft and lightly coloured. Add the mushrooms and fry for a further 1–2 minutes, stirring constantly, then transfer to a bowl.

Drain the mussels, reserving the cooking liquid. Discard the bouquet garni and any mussels which have not opened. Remove all the mussels from their shells, reserving half the shells. Chop the mussels finely, then add to the mushroom mixture with the remaining butter, the parsley and breadcrumbs. Beat well to mix, then stir in 2 × 15 ml spoons/2 tablespoons cream, and pepper to taste.

Divide the mixture equally between the reserved mussel shells, pressing it firmly into each one. Place the shells, stuffed sides facing upward, in individual ovenproof serving dishes.

Strain the reserved cooking liquid and make up to 300 ml/½ pint with wine or water, if necessary. Pour into a clean pan, stir in the remaining cream and pepper to taste, then bring to the boil, stirring.

Pour the sauce carefully around the stuffed mussels, then sprinkle each mussel with a little Parmesan cheese, if using. Bake in a preheated oven for 30 minutes, then serve immediately.

Pâtes d'anchois; Chaussons; Moules farcies à la crème

Crudités avec anchoïade
Raw vegetable hors d'oeuvre

Metric

1 head celery, trimmed,
 with sticks halved
 and cut into even
 lengths
1 small cauliflower,
 divided into florets
4 carrots, peeled and
 cut into thin sticks
½ cucumber, cut into
 sticks, with seeds
 removed
1 large red or green
 pepper, cored, seeded
 and sliced into rings
1 bunch radishes, topped
 and tailed

**Anchoïade
(Anchovy Dip):**

2 × 50 g cans anchovies
 in oil, drained and
 soaked in milk for 20
 minutes
2 tomatoes, skinned,
 seeded and chopped
2 garlic cloves, peeled
 and crushed
1 × 15 ml spoon tomato
 purée
2 × 15 ml spoons wine
 vinegar
about 300 ml olive oil

Imperial

1 head celery, trimmed,
 with sticks halved
 and cut into even
 lengths
1 small cauliflower,
 divided into florets
4 carrots, peeled and
 cut into thin sticks
½ cucumber, cut into
 sticks, with seeds
 removed
1 large red or green
 pepper, cored, seeded,
 and sliced into rings
1 bunch radishes, topped
 and tailed

**Anchoïade
(Anchovy Dip):**

2 × 2 oz cans anchovies
 in oil, drained and
 soaked in milk for 20
 minutes
2 tomatoes, skinned,
 seeded and chopped
2 garlic cloves, peeled
 and crushed
1 tablespoon tomato
 purée
2 tablespoons wine
 vinegar
about ½ pint olive oil

Preparation time: about 50 minutes, plus soaking

It is great fun to serve these crudités and dips for a dinner-party starter, either handing them round with drinks before guests sit down at the table, or serving them as a first course with everything arranged as a centrepiece in the middle of the table. Guests help themselves to the vegetables and a spoonful or two of dip and eat with their fingers. The selection of vegetables can vary according to personal taste and seasonal availability, as long as they are fresh and crisp. Serve the dip suggested here with either a thick homemade mayonnaise or Aïoli (page 9) for contrast. If you enjoy a stronger flavoured anchoïade, use 3 × 50 g/2 oz cans anchovies.

To prepare the anchoïade, drain the anchovies and pat dry with paper towels. Put the anchovies in an electric blender or food processor with the tomatoes, garlic, tomato purée and wine vinegar. Work to a smooth purée, then add the oil a drop at a time until the mixture begins to thicken, as when making mayonnaise. Continue adding the oil in a thin, steady stream until a thick, smooth paste is formed, then turn into a serving bowl. Cover and leave to stand at room temperature until serving time.

To serve, arrange the prepared vegetables in groups in a large salad bowl or basket, with the dip placed around in separate serving bowls or place a bowl of the dip in the centre of a large tray or platter and arrange the groups of vegetables around the outside. Serve immediately the vegetables are prepared or they will lose their crispness.

Tartelettes au chèvre; Crudités avec anchoïade

Tartelettes au chèvre
Goat's cheese tartlets

Preparation time: 30 minutes, plus chilling
Cooking time: 25–30 minutes
Oven: 190°C, 375°F, Gas Mark 5

Metric
125 g plain flour
pinch of salt
100 g butter, chilled
1 egg yolk
1 × 5 ml spoon water
a little beaten egg
    white

Filling:
225 g chèvre (goat's milk
    cheese), rind removed
2 eggs, beaten
2 × 15 ml spoons brandy
    (optional)
1 × 5 ml spoon freshly
chopped thyme or
    1 × 2.5 ml spoon dried
    thyme
1 × 5 ml spoon freshly
chopped marjoram or
    1 × 2.5 ml spoon dried
    marjoram
freshly ground black
    pepper

Imperial
5 oz plain flour
pinch of salt
4 oz butter, chilled
1 egg yolk
1 teaspoon water
a little beaten egg
    white

Filling:
8 oz chèvre (goat's milk
    cheese), rind removed
2 eggs, beaten
2 tablespoons brandy
    (optional)
1 teaspoon freshly
chopped thyme or
    ½ teaspoon dried
    thyme
1 teaspoon freshly
chopped marjoram or
    ½ teaspoon dried
    marjoram
freshly ground black
    pepper

Chèvre, or goat's milk cheese, is available at good Continental delicatessens and some large supermarkets. It makes a strong, flavoursome filling for these tartlets which can be served on their own as a starter or with a selection of salads for lunchtime or a picnic.

To make the pastry, sift the flour and salt into a bowl. Cut the butter into the flour in small pieces, then rub in lightly with the fingertips. Mix the egg yolk and water together, then stir into the flour mixture with a round-bladed knife until the mixture draws together. Form into a smooth ball with one hand, then chill in the refrigerator for 30 minutes.
Meanwhile, make the filling. Put the cheese in a bowl and beat with a wooden spoon until soft and creamy. Beat in the remaining filling ingredients with pepper to taste and set aside.
Roll out the dough on a floured surface and use to line 4 loose-bottomed 10 cm/4 inch flan tins or tartlet moulds. Prick the base of the dough in several places with a fork, then line with foil or greaseproof paper and fill with baking beans.
Bake the pastry cases 'blind' in a preheated oven for 10 minutes, then remove the paper and beans and brush the base of the dough with beaten egg white. Return to the oven and bake for a further 5 minutes. Remove the sides of the tins, then pour the prepared filling into the pastry cases. Bake for 10–15 minutes until the filling is set. Serve warm.

Avocat au crabe
Baked avocado stuffed with crab

Metric
25 g butter
25 g plain flour
300 ml warm milk
salt
1 × 1.25 ml spoon cayenne
 pepper
225 g fresh or frozen
 crabmeat, flaked
2 large ripe avocado pears
juice of ½ lemon

To finish:
25–50 g Gruyère cheese,
 grated
a little cayenne pepper

Imperial
1 oz butter
1 oz plain flour
½ pint warm milk
salt
¼ teaspoon cayenne
 pepper
8 oz fresh or frozen
 crabmeat, flaked
2 large ripe avocado pears
juice of ½ lemon

To finish:
1–2 oz Gruyère cheese,
 grated
a little cayenne pepper

Preparation time: 25 minutes
Cooking time: 20–25 minutes
Oven: 180°C, 350°F, Gas Mark 4

Melt the butter in a pan, stir in the flour and cook for 1–2 minutes, stirring all the time. Remove from the heat and gradually add the milk, beating vigorously after each addition. When all the milk is incorporated, return to the heat and bring slowly to the boil, beating constantly. Lower the heat and simmer until thick, then stir in salt to taste and the cayenne. Remove from the heat, then fold in the flaked crabmeat. Set aside. Halve the avocados, remove the stones and sprinkle the exposed flesh with the lemon juice. Spoon the crab sauce into the avocado cavities and over the top to cover the flesh completely. Stand the avocado shells facing upright in an ovenproof dish. (If they are difficult to stand upright, place each one on a base of crumpled kitchen foil.) Sprinkle the tops with grated cheese, and a little cayenne pepper, then bake in a preheated oven for 15–20 minutes. Transfer carefully to individual serving bowls and serve immediately.

Champignons de Dijon
Mushrooms marinated in mustard

Metric
450 g small white button
 mushrooms
juice of ½ lemon
4 × 15 ml spoons light
 Dijon mustard
4 × 5 ml spoons freshly
 chopped tarragon or
 2 × 5 ml spoons dried
 tarragon
salt
freshly ground black
 pepper
120 ml soured cream
lettuce leaves, to serve

Imperial
1 lb small white button
 mushrooms
juice of ½ lemon
4 tablespoons light Dijon
 mustard
4 teaspoons freshly
 chopped tarragon or
 2 teaspoons dried
 tarragon
salt
freshly ground black
 pepper
4 fl oz soured cream
lettuce leaves, to serve

Preparation time: about 25 minutes, plus marinating

Dijon mustard is a smooth-textured French mustard with a mild flavour. The quantity in this recipe can be adjusted according to taste, but the flavour of the mustard should be predominant. In France, crème fraîche would be used for the dressing rather than soured cream. It is a fresh cream with a high butterfat content and a sharp, slightly cheesy flavour. Soured cream is a good equivalent.

Wipe the mushrooms with a damp cloth, but do not wash them. Halve or slice any large mushrooms.
Put the mushrooms in a bowl and sprinkle with the lemon juice. Add the mustard, half the tarragon, and salt and pepper to taste, then stir gently until the mushrooms are evenly coated in the mustard. Cover and leave to marinate for up to 4 hours.
Line 4 individual serving bowls with lettuce leaves and sprinkle with salt and pepper. Fold all but 4 × 15 ml spoons/4 tablespoons soured cream into the mushrooms, taste and adjust the seasoning, then divide the mixture equally between the dishes.
Top each serving with a spoonful of soured cream and sprinkle with the remaining tarragon. Serve immediately, with hot garlic bread.

Avocat au crabe; Champignons de Dijon; Salade verte au roquefort

Salade verte au roquefort
Green salad with Roquefort dressing

Preparation time: about 20 minutes

Roquefort cheese is available at Continental delicatessens, and some large supermarkets. Otherwise, another French blue cheese with a creamy texture can be substituted, such as Bresse Bleu or blue Brie.

Metric
50 g Roquefort cheese
6 × 15 ml spoons olive oil
2 × 15 ml spoons garlic vinegar
2 × 15 ml spoons double cream (optional)
freshly ground black pepper
½ Webb's or Iceberg lettuce, shredded
¼ curly endive, separated into sprigs

Imperial
2 oz Roquefort cheese
6 tablespoons olive oil
2 tablespoons garlic vinegar
2 tablespoons double cream (optional)
freshly ground black pepper
½ Webb's or Iceberg lettuce, shredded
¼ curly endive, separated into sprigs

To make the dressing, crumble the cheese into a bowl, then mash with a fork, adding the oil a drop at a time to make a paste. Whisk in the vinegar and cream (if using), then add pepper to taste. Set aside in a cool place.

Put the lettuce and endive in a large wide salad bowl and toss until evenly mixed.

Whisk the dressing vigorously, taste and adjust the seasoning, then pour over the salad. Toss with salad servers until the salad is evenly coated with the dressing. Serve immediately.

PÂTÉS AND TERRINES

The French are masters in the art of pâté making – from the coarse-textured pork and liver pâtés heavily laced with garlic, to their elegant and subtly-flavoured fish terrines. The French pâtés and terrines you find in your local shops rarely match the flavour of those made at home, and though they may seem time-consuming to make, your efforts will be well rewarded when you proudly present them to family and friends. Serve the lighter ones as a first course with hot toast, Melba toast or crispbreads and crackers; the more substantial mixtures are best as meals in themselves, for lunches, suppers and picnics with fresh French bread, a bottle of wine and maybe a salad or two.

Top: Pâté de campagne; Below: Terrine de canard à l'orange

Terrine de canard à l'orange
Duck and orange terrine

Metric	Imperial
1 × 2–2.25 kg oven-ready duck	1 × 4½–5 lb oven-ready duck
2 × 15 ml spoons brandy	2 tablespoons brandy
225 g chicken livers	8 oz chicken livers
225 g pork sausagemeat	8 oz pork sausagemeat
50 g fresh white breadcrumbs	2 oz fresh white breadcrumbs
finely grated rind and juice of 1 orange	finely grated rind and juice of 1 orange
6 juniper berries, crushed	6 juniper berries, crushed
1 × 1.25 ml spoon ground allspice	¼ teaspoon ground allspice
salt	salt
freshly ground black pepper	freshly ground black pepper
1 egg, beaten, to bind	1 egg, beaten, to bind
1 orange, thinly sliced	1 orange, thinly sliced

Preparation time: 1–1¼ hours, plus chilling
Cooking time: 1½ hours
Oven: 160°C, 325°F, Gas Mark 3

Bone the duck, removing as much meat as possible from the bones by scraping them with a small, sharp knife. Cut 75–100 g/3–4 oz breast meat into thin slivers, place in a dish and pour over the brandy.
Mince all the remaining duck meat with the liver from the duck and the chicken livers. Place in a bowl with the sausagemeat, mix well, then add the breadcrumbs, orange rind and juice, crushed juniper, allspice, and salt and pepper to taste. Mix well again. Drain the brandy from the slivers of duck and stir the brandy into the mixture. Bind with beaten egg.
Brush a 900 ml/1½ pint terrine or mould lightly with oil. Arrange the orange slices neatly in the base, then spoon in half the minced mixture, packing it down well. Arrange the drained slivers of duck breast evenly over the top, then spoon in the remaining minced mixture and press down firmly.
Cover the mould with lightly oiled foil, then stand it in a bain marie (roasting tin half filled with hot water). Cook in a preheated oven for 1½ hours or until the juices run faintly pink and the terrine has shrunk away from the sides of the mould.
Remove from the bain marie and pour off the excess fat and juices that have collected in the bottom of the mould. Leave until cold, then chill in the refrigerator overnight until firm.
Turn out the terrine carefully on to a serving plate and serve chilled, cut into thick slices.
Serves 6–8

Pâté de campagne
Country-style pâté

Metric	Imperial
8 streaky bacon rashers, rinds removed	8 streaky bacon rashers, rinds removed
450 g pig's liver	1 lb pig's liver
450 g chicken livers	1 lb chicken livers
225 g pork back fat or fatty belly pork	8 oz pork back fat or fatty belly pork
175 g fresh white breadcrumbs	6 oz fresh white breadcrumbs
2 eggs, beaten	2 eggs, beaten
2 garlic cloves, peeled and crushed with 1 × 2.5 ml spoon salt	2 garlic cloves, peeled and crushed with ½ teaspoon salt
75 ml red wine	3 fl oz red wine
2 × 15 ml spoons brandy (optional)	2 tablespoons brandy (optional)
2 × 5 ml spoons freshly chopped thyme or 1 × 5 ml spoon dried thyme	2 teaspoons freshly chopped thyme or 1 teaspoon dried thyme
40–50 g pistachio nuts, coarsely chopped	1½–2 oz pistachio nuts, coarsely chopped
freshly ground black pepper	freshly ground black pepper

Preparation time: 30 minutes, plus cooling and chilling
Cooking time: 2½ hours
Oven: 160°C, 325°F, Gas Mark 3

This is a moist, coarse-textured pâté, perfect spread on chunky slices of French bread.

Brush the inside of a 1 kg/2 lb loaf tin or a 1.2 litre/2 pint earthenware dish with oil. Stretch the bacon rashers with the blade of a knife, then use to line the base and sides of the tin or dish. Set aside.
Mince together the pig's liver, chicken livers and pork, then place in a bowl. Add the remaining ingredients with pepper to taste, and stir well.
Spoon into the prepared tin and level the surface. Cover with foil, then stand the tin in a bain marie (roasting tin half filled with hot water). Bake in a preheated oven for 2½ hours until the pâté and the juices are just faintly pink.
Remove from the oven and pour off the excess fat from the tin, leave until cool, then place heavy weights on top of the foil to press the pâté into a firm shape for slicing. When completely cold, place in the refrigerator and chill overnight.
To serve, run the blade of a knife around the edge of the pâté to release the bacon from the sides of the tin, invert a serving plate on top of the tin, then turn out on to the plate. Serve chilled, cut into thick slices.
Serves 8–10

Jambon persillé
Ham and herbs in wine jelly

Preparation time: about 30 minutes, plus chilling
Cooking time: 10 minutes

Metric	Imperial
1 × 25 g packet aspic jelly powder	1 × 1 oz packet aspic jelly powder
150 ml warm water	¼ pint warm water
300 ml dry white wine	½ pint dry white wine
25 g butter	1 oz butter
2 shallots or 1 small onion, peeled and very finely chopped	2 shallots or 1 small onion, peeled and very finely chopped
1–2 garlic cloves, peeled and crushed	1–2 garlic cloves, peeled and crushed
25 g fresh parsley, very finely chopped	1 oz fresh parsley, very finely chopped
25 g fresh chervil or chives, very finely chopped	1 oz fresh chervil or chives, very finely chopped
freshly ground black pepper	freshly ground black pepper
225–350 g cooked ham, diced	8–12 oz cooked ham, diced
thick Aïoli (page 9), or plain mayonnaise, to serve	thick Aïoli (page 9), or plain mayonnaise, to serve

Dissolve the aspic jelly powder in the warm water and wine according to packet instructions, then leave until cold.

Meanwhile, melt the butter in a pan, add the shallots or onions and garlic, and fry gently until soft and lightly coloured. Remove from the heat, stir in the herbs and pepper, then stir into the liquid aspic jelly. Rinse out a 450 g/1 lb loaf tin with water. Pour in a little of the liquid aspic to cover the bottom of the tin, then chill in the refrigerator for about 30 minutes until just beginning to set.

Place about one-quarter of the ham pieces on top of the layer of aspic jelly, pressing it into the jelly slightly. Return to the refrigerator for a further 30 minutes or until completely set.

Pour another layer of aspic jelly over the ham and continue making and refrigerating these layers, finishing with a layer of jelly. If the jelly in the pan sets during this time, place the pan over gentle heat and stir until the jelly becomes liquid again.

Chill in the refrigerator overnight, then run a sharp knife around the top edge of the tin and unmould on to an inverted serving plate. Serve chilled, with mayonnaise or aïoli handed separately.
Serves 6

Jambon persillé; Galantine de poularde

Galantine de poularde
Boned stuffed chicken

Metric
1 × 1.5 kg oven-ready
  chicken
25 g butter
1 large onion, peeled and
  finely chopped
3 celery sticks, finely
  chopped
225 g chicken livers,
  roughly chopped
175 g button mushrooms,
  finely chopped
4 rashers back bacon, rind
  removed, roughly
  chopped
100 g fresh white
  breadcrumbs
2 × 15 ml spoons freshly
  chopped parsley
1 × 5 ml spoon dried
  mixed herbs
finely grated rind of 1
  lemon
salt
freshly ground black
  pepper
1 egg, beaten
1 garlic clove, peeled and
  halved
juice of ½ lemon

Imperial
1 × 3½ lb oven-ready
  chicken
1 oz butter
1 large onion, peeled and
  finely chopped
3 celery sticks, finely
  chopped
8 oz chicken livers,
  roughly chopped
6 oz button mushrooms,
  finely chopped
4 rashers back bacon, rind
  removed, roughly
  chopped
4 oz fresh white
  breadcrumbs
2 tablespoons freshly
  chopped parsley
1 teaspoon dried mixed
  mixed herbs
finely grated rind of 1
  lemon
salt
freshly ground black
  pepper
1 egg, beaten
1 garlic clove, peeled and
  halved
juice of ½ lemon

Preparation time: 1¼ hours, plus cooling and chilling
Cooking time: 2¼ hours
Oven: 180°C, 350°F, Gas Mark 4

Put the chicken on a board or work surface, breast side down. With a sharp, pointed knife, cut down the back of the bird, working from the neck to the tail end to expose the backbone. Scrape the flesh away from the carcass on one side of the backbone, keeping the knife facing towards the bones, not the flesh. Scrape down to the ball joint of the leg, then repeat on the other side of the carcass. Bone the legs by cutting through the sinew that joins them to the carcass, then scraping away all the flesh from the main leg bone, holding it firmly by the tip and working down to meet the carcass at the ball joint. Discard all bones from the legs. Bone the wings in the same way, cutting them through at the point where they join the body. Continue scraping away the flesh from the carcass and rib cage of the bird until the breastbone at the front is reached on both sides. Remove the carcass by carefully cutting along the breastbone, taking great care not to slit the thin flesh or skin over the breastbone.

Melt the butter in a pan, add the onion and celery and fry gently until lightly coloured. Stir in the chicken livers and mushrooms and fry for a further 5 minutes, stirring constantly, then transfer to a bowl. Add the bacon, breadcrumbs, parsley, herbs, lemon rind, and salt and pepper to taste. Mix well together, then bind with the beaten egg.

Lay the chicken flat on the board or work surface, skin side down. Place the stuffing mixture in the centre, shaping it with your hands into a neat rectangle. Wrap the chicken around the stuffing to make a neat parcel shape, tucking the legs and wings inside. Sew with thread or fine string, then place on a rack in a roasting tin. Rub the cut surfaces of the garlic all over the skin of the chicken, then sprinkle with the lemon juice and salt and pepper. Cover with foil and roast in a preheated oven for 2 hours, removing the foil for the last 30 minutes to brown the skin. Leave to go cold.

Wrap tightly in cling film or foil, then chill in the refrigerator overnight. Remove the thread or string, then slice neatly.
Serves 8

Terrine de légumes
Courgette and spinach terrine

Preparation time: about 1 hour
Cooking time: about 1¾ hours
Oven: 160°C, 325°F, Gas Mark 3

Metric
2 × 15 ml spoons olive oil
1 onion, peeled and thinly
  sliced
350 g courgettes, sliced
350 g frozen chopped
  spinach, thawed
salt
freshly ground black
  pepper
1 × 2.5 ml spoon freshly
  grated nutmeg
225 g curd cheese
50 g fresh white
  breadcrumbs
2 × 5 ml spoons freshly
  chopped basil or 1 × 5
  ml spoon dried basil
2 × 5 ml spoons freshly
  chopped marjoram or
  1 × 5 ml spoon dried
  marjoram (optional)
1 egg, beaten
melted butter for greasing
  tin

Imperial
2 tablespoons olive oil
1 onion, peeled and thinly
  sliced
12 oz courgettes, sliced
12 oz frozen chopped
  spinach, thawed
salt
freshly ground black
  pepper
½ teaspoon freshly
  grated nutmeg
8 oz curd cheese
2 oz fresh white
  breadcrumbs
2 teaspoons freshly
  chopped basil or 1
  teaspoon dried basil
2 teaspoons freshly
  chopped marjoram or
  1 teaspoon dried
  marjoram (optional)
1 egg, beaten
melted butter for greasing
  tin

Heat the oil in a frying pan, add the onion and courgettes and fry gently until soft and lightly coloured. Remove from the pan with a slotted spoon, then place in a single layer on paper towels. Cover with more paper towels and press to remove excess oil.

Put the spinach in a heavy-based pan and heat gently until thoroughly dry, stirring frequently. Remove from the heat and stir in generous amounts of salt, pepper and the nutmeg.

Work the courgettes and onions to a purée in an electric blender or vegetable mill, then place in a heavy-based pan and dry out over gentle heat as with the spinach. Transfer to a bowl, then beat in the curd cheese, breadcrumbs, basil, marjoram (if using), and salt and pepper to taste. Bind with the beaten egg.

Brush the inside of a 450 g/1 lb loaf tin liberally with butter, line the base with greaseproof paper, then brush with more butter. Put half the courgette mixture in the bottom of the tin, pressing it down firmly and levelling the surface. Spread the spinach in an even layer over the top, then press in the remaining courgette mixture.

Cover the tin with buttered foil, then stand it in a bain marie (roasting tin half filled with hot water) and bake in a preheated oven for 1¼ hours or until the mixture feels firm and set when a knife is inserted in the centre.

Remove from the bain marie, leave the terrine in the tin until completely cold, then chill in the refrigerator overnight until firm.

Loosen the sides of the terrine from the tin with a knife, then carefully turn out on to a serving plate and peel off the greaseproof paper. Serve chilled, cut into thick slices.
Serves 6

Terrine de légumes; Rillettes de porc

Rillettes de porc
Potted pork

Preparation time: about 45 minutes, plus chilling
Cooking time: 5 hours
Oven: 150°C, 300°F, Gas Mark 2;
140°C, 275°F, Gas Mark 1

Metric	Imperial
1.25 kg belly pork, boned and rind removed	*2½ lb belly pork, boned and rind removed*
225 g pork back fat	*8 oz pork back fat*
120 ml water	*4 fl oz water*
2 garlic cloves, peeled and crushed with 1 × 2.5 ml spoon salt	*2 garlic cloves, peeled and crushed with ½ teaspoon salt*
1 × 2.5 ml spoon ground allspice	*½ teaspoon ground allspice*
freshly ground black pepper	*freshly bround black pepper*
1 bouquet garni	*1 bouquet garni*
1 bay leaf	*1 bay leaf*

Rillettes de porc are a familiar sight in charcuteries all over France, although they are a speciality of the Loire region. Although slightly tricky to prepare, served with crusty French bread they make an excellent lunch or picnic dish. The proportion of pork to fat can be varied according to individual taste.
Stored in the refrigerator with the seal of fat unbroken, rillettes keep for up to 2 weeks.

Cut the belly pork and back fat into small 5 mm/¼ inch cubes and place in an earthenware casserole dish. Add the water, garlic, allspice and pepper to taste. Stir well to mix, then bury the bouquet garni and bay leaf in the centre.
Cover the casserole tightly with a lid, then cook in a preheated oven for 2½ hours. Reduce the oven temperature and cook for a further 2½ hours. Stir occasionally to prevent the pork or fat sticking.
After 5 hours' cooking, tip the contents of the casserole into a sieve standing over a bowl. Discard the bouquet garni and bay leaf and any large pieces of solid fat, then shred the meat thoroughly with the forks (it should be so soft and tender that it will literally fall apart). Taste and adjust the seasoning.
Pack the shredded meat tightly into 4 individual ramekin dishes, pressing it down firmly with the back of a metal spoon. Leave the strained fat and juices in the bowl until cool and just beginning to thicken, then pour over the top of the meat, leaving behind any sediment that has settled at the bottom of the bowl. Leave until completely cold, by which time the fat will have solidified on top of the meat to seal it, then chill in the refrigerator overnight before serving.

EGGS, CHEESE AND FISH

At lunchtime the French often eat a simple omelette or quiche with bread and a salad. Together with their hundreds of regional cheeses to choose from, there is no lack of variation on this midday theme.

Fresh fish in France is a joy to eat; shellfish from Normandy and Brittany, oysters and mussels from breeding ground bordering on the Atlantic, seawater fish from the Mediterranean, and an abundance of freshwater fish from the many inland rivers and streams. For everyday meals fish is cooked as simply as possible, usually grilled or fried in butter then sprinkled with herbs, freshly ground pepper and lemon juice.

Truite au vin blanc
Trout with white wine

Metric	Imperial
4 × 225 g frozen rainbow trout, defrosted	*4 × 8 oz frozen rainbow trout, defrosted*
4 bay leaves	*4 bay leaves*
2 lemons, thinly sliced	*2 lemons, thinly sliced*
salt	*salt*
freshly ground black pepper	*freshly ground black pepper*
300 ml dry white wine	*½ pint dry white wine*
juice of 1 lemon	*juice of 1 lemon*
150 ml double cream	*¼ pint double cream*
1 × 15 ml spoon light Dijon mustard	*1 tablespoon light Dijon mustard*
1–2 × 15 ml spoons freshly chopped parsley	*1–2 tablespoons freshly chopped parsley*

To garnish:	**To garnish:**
few lemon slices	*few lemon slices*
few parsley sprigs	*few parsley sprigs*

Preparation time: 15 minutes
Cooking time: about 40–45 minutes
Oven: 160°C, 325°F, Gas Mark 3

Wash the trout inside and out under cold running water, then pat dry with paper towels. Place in a single layer in a buttered flameproof dish. Insert 1 bay leaf and a few lemon slices inside each fish.

Sprinkle the fish with salt and pepper, then pour over the wine, adding enough water just to cover the fish. Cover with foil and bake in a preheated oven for 20–25 minutes until the fish flakes easily when tested with a fork.

Drain the liquid from the fish into a heavy-based pan. Remove the lemon and bay leaves, place the fish on a warmed serving platter, cover with foil and keep warm in the lowest possible oven.

Stir the lemon juice into the liquid in the pan. Bring to the boil and boil vigorously until the liquid is reduced by about one-third of its volume. Stir in the cream and continue boiling for a further 5–10 minutes until the sauce is thickened and just beginning to turn golden, whisking continuously with a wire balloon whisk. Remove from the heat and add the mustard, parsley and salt and pepper to taste.

Pour a little sauce over the fish, and garnish with lemon slices and parsley. Serve immediately, with the remaining sauce in a warmed sauceboat.

Timbale au jambon
Pasta mould with ham

Metric
150 g macaroni
salt
50 g butter
50 g plain flour
450 ml warm milk
100 g Gruyère cheese, grated
2 eggs
1 egg yolk
2 × 15 ml spoons freshly chopped parsley
freshly ground black pepper
100 g boiled ham, diced

Imperial
5 oz macaroni
salt
2 oz butter
2 oz plain flour
¾ pint warm milk
4 oz Gruyère cheese, grated
2 eggs
1 egg yolk
2 tablespoons freshly chopped parsley
freshly ground black pepper
4 oz boiled ham, diced

Tomato sauce:
2 × 15 ml spoons olive oil
1 small onion, peeled and chopped
2 garlic cloves, peeled and crushed with 1 × 2.5 ml spoon salt
350 g tomatoes, skinned, seeded and chopped
2 × 15 ml spoons tomato purée
pinch of sugar
300 ml dry white wine or water

Tomato sauce:
2 tablespoons olive oil
1 small onion, peeled and chopped
2 garlic cloves, peeled and crushed with ½ teaspoon salt
12 oz tomatoes, skinned, seeded and chopped
2 tablespoons tomato purée
pinch of sugar
½ pint dry white wine or water

From left: Timbale au jambon; Truite au vin blanc

Preparation time: 30 minutes
Cooking time: about 1½ hours
Oven: 190°C, 375°F, Gas Mark 5

Cook the macaroni in boiling salted water for about 8 minutes until 'al dente' (tender yet firm to the bite). Drain thoroughly, then rinse under cold running water. Leave to drain.

Meanwhile, melt the butter in a pan, stir in the flour and cook for 1–2 minutes, stirring all the time. Remove from the heat and gradually add the milk, beating vigorously. Return the pan to the heat and bring slowly to the boil, beating constantly. Lower the heat and simmer until thick, then add the cheese and heat gently until melted.

Leave the sauce to cool slightly, then stir in the whole eggs and egg yolk, parsley, and salt and pepper.

Combine the macaroni and sauce, then fold in the ham. Turn the mixture into a well-buttered 900 ml/1½ pint charlotte or savavin mould, pressing it down firmly and levelling the surface. Cover with foil, then bake in a preheated oven for 50 minutes or until set.

Meanwhile, make the tomato sauce. Heat the oil in a pan, add the onion and garlic and fry gently until soft. Stir in the tomatoes, tomato purée, sugar and salt and pepper, and fry for a further 5 minutes, stirring constantly. Stir in the wine or water and bring to the boil, then lower the heat and simmer gently for 20 minutes, stirring occasionally.

Allow the sauce to cool slightly, then purée in an electric blender or work through a sieve. Return to the rinsed-out pan and heat through gently. Adjust the consistency of the sauce – if it is too thick, stir in more wine or water, if too thin, boil vigorously until reduced. Taste and adjust the seasoning.

Remove the mould from the oven and leave to stand in a warm place for 10 minutes. Unmould on to a warmed serving platter and pour over a little of the tomato sauce. Serve immediately, with the remaining sauce handed separately in a warmed sauceboat.

Soupe de poissons marseillaise
Marseille fish soup

Preparation time: about 25 minutes
Cooking time: 30 minutes

Metric	*Imperial*
2 × 15 ml spoons olive oil	2 tablespoons olive oil
1 large onion, peeled and thinly sliced	1 large onion, peeled and thinly sliced
2 tomatoes, skinned, seeded and chopped	2 tomatoes, skinned, seeded and chopped
1 × 15 ml spoon tomato purée	1 tablespoon tomato purée
1 litre fish stock	2 pints fish stock
300 ml dry white wine	½ pint dry white wine
1 bay leaf	1 bay leaf
1 strip orange peel	1 strip orange peel
1 sprig fresh fennel or 1 × 5 ml spoon dried fennel	1 sprig fresh fennel or 1 teaspoon dried fennel
salt	salt
freshly ground black pepper	freshly ground black pepper
1 kg mixed white fish (e.g., mullet, cod, haddock, plaice, turbot), skinned, boned and cut into chunks	2 lb mixed white fish (e.g., mullet, cod, haddock, plaice, turbot), skinned, boned and cut into chunks
100 g peeled prawns (optional)	4 oz peeled prawns (optional)
150 ml Aïoli (page 9)	¼ pint Aïoli (page 9)
slices of hot toast, to serve	slices of hot toast, to serve

As this recipe requires a mixture of white fish you can ask the fishmonger for the fish heads and tails to make the stock. If you are buying ready-prepared or frozen fish and have no trimmings to make stock, chicken stock may be substituted.

In France the broth from a soup such as this one is served as a first course. Each person helps himself to toast, and pours the broth over the toast in his own plate. The aïoli is stirred in according to individual taste. The fish is then eaten separately as a main course, with more aïoli.

Heat the oil in a large flameproof casserole or heavy-based pan. Add the onion and fry gently until soft Stir in the tomatoes and tomato purée and fry for a further 5 minutes, stirring constantly.

Stir in the fish stock and wine and bring to the boil. Lower the heat, add the bay leaf, orange peel, fennel, and salt and pepper. Add the firm fleshed white fish (such as cod, haddock and mullet), and simmer for 10 minutes, then add the more delicate fish (such as plaice and turbot). Simmer for a further 5 minutes, then add the prawns, if using, and continue cooking for a further 5 minutes, until all the fish is tender and flakes easily when tested with a fork.

To serve, remove the bay leaf, orange peel and fennel sprig (if using). Taste and adjust the seasoning of the soup, then transfer to a warmed tureen or individual plates. Serve immediately, handing round the aïoli separately and served with toast.

Matafam
Cheese and bacon pancake

Preparation time: 25 minutes, plus 30 minutes for standing
Cooking time: about 15 minutes

Metric	*Imperial*
100 g plain flour	4 oz plain flour
pinch of salt	pinch of salt
4 eggs, beaten	4 eggs, beaten
100 g Gruyère cheese, grated	4 oz Gruyère cheese, grated
100 g streaky bacon, rinds removed, cut into strips	4 oz streaky bacon, rinds removed, cut into strips
freshly grated nutmeg	freshly grated nutmeg
salt	salt
freshly ground black pepper	freshly ground black pepper
50 g butter	2 oz butter

Originally a Spanish dish, the word matafam means 'to kill hunger' in Catalan. Serve hot with fried eggs, grilled bacon or sausages as a lunch or brunch dish, or cold with pickles, cooked meats and cheeses.

Sift the flour and salt into a bowl and make a well in the centre. Put the eggs in the well with the cheese and bacon, then gradually work in the flour with a wooden spoon, drawing it in from the sides of the bowl until evenly mixed. Add nutmeg, salt and pepper to taste, then cover and leave the batter at room temperature for 30 minutes.

Melt half the butter in a heavy-based crêpe or frying pan. Pour in the batter and fry over moderate heat for 7 minutes until the underside is set and golden.

Meanwhile, melt the remaining butter in a separate pan. Drizzle evenly over the top of the matafam, then slide the pan under a preheated hot grill and cook for about 5 minutes until the top is golden brown. Serve immediately, cut into wedges.

From left: Matafam: Soupe de poissons marseillaise; La râpée

La râpée
Egg and grated potato gratin

Preparation time: 20–25 minutes
Cooking time: 35–40 minutes
Oven: 200°C, 400°F, Gas Mark 6

Metric	Imperial
50 g butter	*2 oz butter*
2 × 15 ml spoons olive oil	*2 tablespoons olive oil*
2 shallots or 1 small onion, peeled and finely chopped	*2 shallots or 1 small onion, peeled and finely chopped*
1 garlic clove, peeled and crushed with 1 × 2.5 ml spoon salt	*1 garlic clove, peeled and crushed with ½ teaspoon salt*
4 eggs	*4 eggs*
150 ml double cream	*¼ pint double cream*
100 g Gruyère cheese, grated	*4 oz Gruyère cheese, grated*
salt	*salt*
freshly ground black pepper	*freshly ground black pepper*
4 medium potatoes, peeled	*4 medium potatoes, peeled*

Such dishes, known as 'gratins' in France, are popular for light lunches or suppers, and can be made with different vegetables such as leeks and chicory. Sometimes, ham and anchovies are added for extra flavour and body.

Melt half the butter with the oil in a pan, add the shallots and garlic and fry gently until soft. Transfer to a bowl, add the eggs and beat well. Stir in the cream, Gruyère cheese, salt and pepper. Set aside.
Grate the potatoes coarsely, squeeze them with your hands to extract as much moisture as possible, then pat dry with paper towels. Stir into the egg mixture.
Put the remaining butter in a shallow ovenproof dish and heat in a preheated oven until melted and very hot.
Pour in the egg and potato mixture, then bake for 25–30 minutes or until firm, with a crisp golden crust on top. Serve immediately.

Gougère aux foies de volailles
Choux pastry ring with chicken livers

Metric
300 ml water
100 g butter, cut into
   small pieces
salt
150 g plain flour
4 eggs, beaten
100 g Gruyère cheese,
   grated
about 1 × 1.25 ml spoon
   cayenne pepper

Filling:
25 g butter
1 medium onion, peeled
   and thinly sliced
1–2 garlic cloves, peeled
   and crushed with 1 ×
   2.5 ml spoon salt
225 g chicken livers, sliced
2 × 5 ml spoons freshly
   chopped marjoram or 1
   × 5 ml spoon dried
   marjoram
1 × 5 ml spoon tomato
   purée
4 × 15 ml spoons dry
   sherry
4 × 15 ml spoons single
   cream
freshly chopped parsley,
   to garnish

Imperial
½ pint water
4 oz butter, cut into small
   pieces
salt
5 oz plain flour
4 eggs, beaten
4 oz Gruyère cheese,
   grated
about ¼ teaspoon cayenne
   pepper

Filling:
1 oz butter
1 medium onion, peeled
   and thinly sliced
1–2 garlic cloves, peeled
   and crushed with ½
   teaspoon salt
8 oz chicken livers, sliced
2 teaspoons freshly
   chopped marjoram or 1
   teaspoon dried
   marjoram
1 teaspoon tomato
   purée
4 tablespoons dry
   sherry
4 tablespoons single
   cream
freshly chopped parsley,
   to garnish

Preparation time: about 30 minutes
Cooking time: 45–50 minutes
Oven: 200°C, 400°F, Gas Mark 6

Put the water in a large heavy-based pan with the pieces of butter and a pinch of salt. Bring to the boil, then remove from the heat and add the flour all at once. Return to gentle heat and beat vigorously with a wooden spoon until the mixture forms a ball and leaves the sides of the pan clean.

Remove from the heat and gradually beat in the eggs, until the mixture becomes smooth and glossy, reserving a little egg for glazing. Beat in the grated cheese and salt, and cayenne to taste.

Place spoonfuls of the dough on a greased baking sheet to make a circle or crown shape 20–23 cm/8–9 inches in diameter. Brush with the reserved beaten egg, then bake in a preheated oven for 30–35 minutes until puffed up and golden brown.

Meanwhile make the filling. Melt the butter in a frying pan, add the onion and garlic and fry gently until soft. Add the chicken livers and fry until lightly coloured on all sides, then stir in the marjoram and tomato purée. Fry for 1–2 minutes, then stir in the sherry and continue cooking for a further 5 minutes, or until the chicken livers are cooked to your liking. Add salt, then stir in the cream and heat through gently without boiling.

When the gougère is cooked, transfer carefully to a warmed serving platter and spoon the chicken liver filling in the centre. Sprinkle with parsley and serve immediately.

Gougère aux foies de volailles; Quiche au camembert

Quiche au camembert
Camembert quiche

Preparation time: about 40 minutes, plus chilling
Cooking time: about 45 minutes
Oven: 190°C, 350°F, Gas Mark 5

Metric
175 g plain flour
pinch of salt
100 g butter, chilled
1 egg yolk
1 × 5 ml spoon water
a little egg white, lightly
    beaten

Imperial
6 oz plain flour
pinch of salt
4 oz butter, chilled
1 egg yolk
1 teaspoon water
a little egg white, lightly
    beaten

Filling:
350 g soft ripe Camembert
    cheese, rind removed
2 eggs, beaten
150 ml double cream
salt
freshly ground black
    pepper

Filling:
12 oz soft ripe Camembert
    cheese, rind removed
2 eggs, beaten
¼ pint double cream
salt
freshly ground black
    pepper

This quiche can equally well be made with Brie cheese. Many supermarkets and delicatessens sell a blue-veined Brie which would make a stronger-tasting filling than plain Brie or Camembert.

To make the pastry, sift the flour and salt into a bowl. Cut the butter into the flour in small pieces, then rub in lightly with the fingertips. Mix the egg yolk and water together, then stir into the flour mixture with a round-bladed knife until the mixture draws together. Form into a smooth ball with one hand, then chill in the refrigerator for 30 minutes.
Roll out the dough on a floured surface and use to line a loose-bottomed 23 cm/9 inch fluted flan tin. Place the tin on a baking sheet, prick the base of the dough in several places with a fork, then line with foil or greaseproof paper and fill with baking beans. Bake the pastry case 'blind' in a preheated oven for 10 minutes, then remove the paper and beans and brush the base with the beaten egg white. Return to the oven and bake for a further 5 minutes then carefully remove the sides of the flan tin. Set the pastry case aside on the baking sheet.
To make the filling, cut the Camembert cheese into small pieces and place in a heatproof bowl. Stand the bowl in a pan of gently simmering water and heat gently, stirring constantly until the cheese has melted and is runny. Remove the bowl from the pan of water and gradually stir in the beaten eggs and cream until evenly mixed. Add a little salt, and pepper to taste.
Pour the filling into the pastry case, return to the oven and bake for 20 minutes or until the filling is puffed up and golden brown. Remove from the oven, quickly place on a serving plate and serve immediately.

Quiche au crabe
Crab quiche

Preparation time: about 40 minutes, plus chilling
Cooking time: about 50 minutes
Oven: 190°C, 375°F, Gas Mark 5

Metric
125 g plain flour
pinch of salt
100 g butter, chilled
1 egg yolk
1 × 5 ml spoon lemon juice
a little egg white, lightly
  beaten

Filling:
25 g unsalted butter
1 onion, peeled and finely
  chopped
1 × 15 ml spoon tomato
  purée
225 g fresh or frozen
  crabmeat, flaked
3 eggs
150 ml milk
salt
cayenne pepper

Imperial
5 oz plain flour
pinch of salt
4 oz butter, chilled
1 egg yolk
1 teaspoon lemon juice
a little egg white, lightly
  beaten

Filling:
1 oz unsalted butter
1 onion, peeled and finely
  chopped
1 tablespoon tomato
  purée
8 oz fresh or frozen
  crabmeat, flaked
3 eggs
¼ pint milk
salt
cayenne pepper

Sift the flour and salt into a bowl. Cut the butter into the flour in small pieces, then rub in lightly with the fingertips. Mix the egg yolk and lemon juice together, then stir into the flour mixture with a round-bladed knife until the mixture draws together. Form into a smooth ball, then chill in the refrigerator for 30 minutes.

Roll out the dough on a floured surface and use to line a plain 20 cm/8 inch flan ring set on a baking sheet. Prick the base of the dough in several places with a fork, then line with foil or greaseproof paper and fill with baking beans.

Bake the pastry case 'blind' in a preheated oven for 10 minutes, then remove the paper and beans and brush the base of the dough with the beaten egg white. Return to the oven and bake for a further 5 minutes, then remove and set aside.

To make the filling, melt the butter in a pan, add the onion and fry gently until soft. Transfer to a bowl and stir in the tomato purée and flaked crabmeat. In a separate bowl, lightly beat the eggs together with the milk and salt and cayenne to taste. Pour over the crabmeat mixture and fold gently to mix.

Pour the filling into the pastry case, then return to the oven and bake for 25 minutes until the filling is just set. Remove the flan ring carefully, then return to the oven for a further 5 minutes to crisp up the edges of the pastry. Leave to cool for about 15 minutes, then transfer the quiche to a serving plate. Serve warm or cold.

Tarte aux oignons
Onion tart

Metric
25 g butter
4 medium Spanish onions,
  peeled and thinly sliced
1 × 5 ml spoon soft brown
  sugar
2 × 15 ml spoons plain
  flour
1 × 15 ml spoon brandy
  (optional)
1 egg
2 egg yolks
4 × 15 ml spoons double
  cream
salt
freshly ground black
  pepper

Pastry:
125 g plain flour
pinch of salt
100 g butter, chilled
1 egg yolk
1 × 5 ml spoon water
a little egg white, lightly
  beaten

Imperial
1 oz butter
4 medium Spanish onions,
  peeled and thinly sliced
1 teaspoon soft brown
  sugar
2 tablespoons plain
  flour
1 tablespoon brandy
  (optional)
1 egg
2 egg yolks
4 tablespoons double
  cream
salt
freshly ground black
  pepper

Pastry:
5 oz plain flour
pinch of salt
4 oz butter, chilled
1 egg yolk
1 teaspoon water
a little egg white, lightly
  beaten

Preparation time: about 40 minutes, plus chilling
Cooking time: about 2 hours
Oven: 190°C, 375°F, Gas Mark 5

Melt the butter in a large heavy-based pan, add the onions and fry very gently for about 1 hour until very soft and golden (almost a puréed consistency). Stir the onions frequently during frying to prevent them from browning and sticking to the pan.

Meanwhile, make the pastry. Sift the flour and salt into a bowl. Cut the butter into the flour in small pieces, then rub in lightly with the fingertips. Mix the egg yolk and water together, then stir into the flour mixture with a round-bladed knife until the mixture draws together. Form into a smooth ball with one hand, then cover and chill in the refrigerator for 30 minutes.

Roll out the dough on a floured surface and use to line a 20 cm/8 inch flan tin or flan ring set on a baking sheet. Prick the base of the dough in several places with a fork, then line with foil or greaseproof paper and fill with baking beans.

Bake the pastry case 'blind' in a preheated oven for 10 minutes, then remove the paper and beans and brush the base of the dough with the beaten egg white. Return to the oven and bake for a further 5 minutes. Set aside. When the onions are cooked, stir in the sugar and cook for 1 minute, then sprinkle in the flour and cook for a further 2 minutes, stirring constantly with a wooden spoon.

Transfer the onions to a bowl and stir in the brandy (if using). Beat the whole egg and egg yolks together, then stir into the onions with the cream and salt and pepper to taste.

Pour the filling into the pastry case, then place in the oven and bake for 30–35 minutes until the filling is set. Leave to cool for about 15 minutes, then remove the flan tin or ring and place the quiche on a serving plate. Serve warm or cold.

Quiche au crabe; Tarte aux oignons

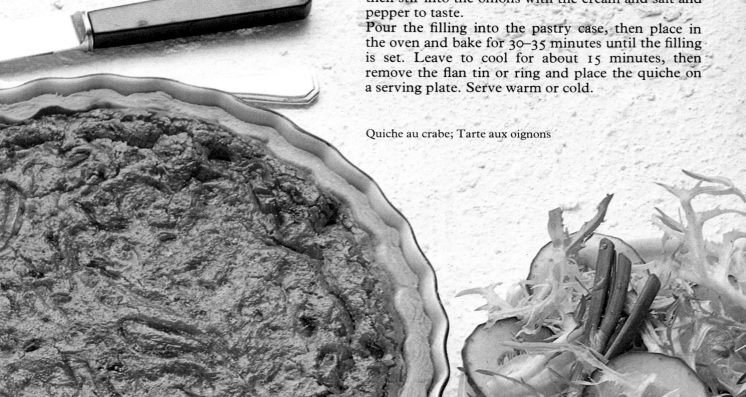

Sardines grillées à l'ail
Grilled sardines with garlic

Metric	Imperial
I kg (about 30) fresh sardines	*2 lb (about 30) fresh sardines*
6 × 15 ml spoons olive oil	*6 tablespoons olive oil*
juice of I lemon	*juice of I lemon*
4 garlic cloves, peeled and crushed with I × 5 ml spoon salt	*4 garlic cloves, peeled and crushed with I teaspoon salt*
2 × 15 ml spoons finely chopped parsley	*2 tablespoons finely chopped parsley*
freshly ground black pepper	*freshly ground black pepper*
lemon wedges, to serve	*lemon wedges, to serve*

Preparation time: 30 minutes, plus marinating
Cooking time: about 8 minutes

In France, fresh sardines are often cooked over charcoal and are usually left whole, with the heads on; for English tastes, they are more palatable if gutted and cleaned before cooking.
Serve for a light lunch dish (cooked on the barbecue in summer) with French bread or garlic bread, and a tossed green salad or tomato, basil and onion salad, and a thick plain, or garlic-flavoured mayonnaise such as Aïoli (page 9). For a starter, serve with bread and mayonnaise only, and allow 4–6 sardines for each person.

To gut and clean the sardines: insert the point of a small, sharp knife in the centre of the belly and cut along the belly to the gills. Cut off the head behind the gills, gently pulling the entrails of the fish away with it. Cut along the belly towards the tail, then gently open out the fish. Locate the backbone at the head end with the point of the knife, and gently ease it away from the flesh. With thumb and forefinger, pull the backbone away towards the tail. Cut off the backbone with the tail.
Rinse the sardines inside and out under gently running water, then pat dry with paper towels. Place in a single layer in a shallow dish. Mix together the remaining ingredients with plenty of pepper, then pour over the fish. Leave to marinate for at least I hour, turning the fish over frequently.
Place the sardines in a single layer on a grill rack covered with foil. Reserve the marinade. Cook under a preheated hot grill for about 4 minutes on each side or until the skin is charred and the flesh cooked through each side, basting frequently with the reserved marinade. Transfer to warmed individual serving plates and pour over the pan juices and any remaining marinade. Serve immediately, with lemon wedges.

Maquereau en concombre vinaigrette
Mackerel in creamy vinaigrette

Metric	Imperial
4 mackerel (about 275 g each), gutted	*4 mackerel (about 10 oz each), gutted*
salt	*salt*
freshly ground black pepper	*freshly ground black pepper*
½ large cucumber, thinly sliced	*½ large cucumber, thinly sliced*
juice of I lemon	*juice of I lemon*
50 g unsalted butter	*2 oz unsalted butter*

Dressing:	**Dressing:**
120 ml olive oil	*4 fl oz olive oil*
3 × 15 ml spoons cider vinegar	*3 tablespoons cider vinegar*
2 × 15 ml spoons Aïoli (page 9) or plain mayonnaise	*2 tablespoons Aïoli (page 9) or plain mayonnaise*
2 × 15 ml spoons freshly chopped parsley	*2 tablespoons freshly chopped parsley*

Preparation time: 20–30 minutes
Cooking time: 25–30 minutes
Oven: 200°C, 400°F, Gas Mark 6

Place each mackerel on a piece of foil. Sprinkle the insides of the fish with salt and pepper, then tuck the cucumber inside, reserving a few slices for the garnish. Sprinkle more salt and pepper over the tops of the mackerel, pour over the lemon juice and dot with the butter.
Fold the foil over the fish, tucking in the ends to make 4 individual parcels. Place the fish in a single layer in a large baking dish and bake in a preheated oven for 25–30 minutes or until the fish is cooked through.
Meanwhile, make the dressing. Put all the ingredients in a screw-topped jar with salt and pepper to taste. Shake well to mix, then chill in the refrigerator.
When the mackerel are cooked, unwrap carefully, drain off all the cooking juices and place the fish on a warmed serving platter. Pour over the chilled dressing and serve immediately, garnished with the reserved cucumber twists and accompanied by slices of bread.

From the top: Maquereau en concombre vinaigrette; Sardines grillées à l'ail; Coquilles au cidre

Coquilles au cidre
Scallops with cider

Metric	Imperial
8 scallops (total weight about 350 g), defrosted if frozen	8 scallops (total weight about 12 oz), defrosted if frozen
100 g button mushrooms, finely sliced	4 oz button mushrooms, finely sliced
300 ml dry cider	½ pint dry cider
1 bay leaf, halved	1 bay leaf, halved
2 shallots or 1 small onion, peeled and finely chopped	2 shallots or 1 small onion, peeled and finely chopped
cayenne pepper	cayenne pepper
salt	salt
150 ml double cream	¼ pint double cream
40 g butter	1½ oz butter
40 g fresh white breadcrumbs	1½ oz fresh white breadcrumbs
40 g Gruyère cheese, grated	1½ oz Gruyère cheese, grated

Preparation time: about 30 minutes
Cooking time: about 35 minutes

If using fresh scallops, scrub and scald the shells, for 1 minute in boiling water with 1 × 5 ml spoon/1 teaspoon lemon juice. Frozen scallop meat is available off the shell from good freezer centres, supermarkets and fishmongers. Empty scallop shells (for serving) can be obtained from fishmongers or bought at specialist kitchen shops.

Wash the scallops and coral thoroughly under cold running water, then slice thinly. Put them in a pan with the mushrooms, cider, bay leaf, shallots or onion and a pinch each of cayenne and salt. Bring to the boil, then skim off the scum with a slotted spoon and lower the heat. Simmer gently for 4–6 minutes until the scallops are tender, then strain the liquid into a clean pan, discarding the bay leaf halves.
Boil the liquid vigorously until reduced by about half of its volume. Stir in the cream and continue boiling for a further 5–10 minutes until the sauce is thickened and just beginning to turn golden, whisking continuously with a wire ballon whisk.
Meanwhile, divide the scallops and coral mixture equally between 4 buttered scallop shells. When the sauce is thick, remove from the heat and whisk in half the butter. Taste and adjust the seasoning, then pour over the scallop mixture.
Mix together the breadcrumbs and cheese and sprinkle evenly over the scallops. Dot with the remaining butter and sprinkle with cayenne to taste. Put under a preheated hot grill for about 5 minutes until golden brown and bubbling. Serve hot.

Moules en brochette
Mussel kebabs

Metric	Imperial
1.5–1.75 kg fresh mussels, scrubbed, with beards removed	3–4 lb fresh mussels, scrubbed, with beards removed
150 ml dry white wine	¼ pint dry white wine
150 ml water	¼ pint water
1 medium onion, peeled and chopped	1 medium onion, peeled and chopped
1 bouquet garni	1 bouquet garni
225 g unsmoked back bacon, rind removed, cut into chunks, or bacon rashers, cut into lengths and folded double	8 oz unsmoked back bacon, rind removed, cut into chunks, or bacon rashers, cut into lengths and folded double
1 red pepper, cored, seeded, and cut into chunks	1 red pepper, cored, seeded, and cut into chunks
1 green pepper, cored, seeded and cut into chunks	1 green pepper, cored, seeded and cut into chunks
100 g unsalted butter, softened	4 oz unsalted butter, softened
2 garlic cloves, peeled and crushed	2 garlic cloves, peeled and crushed
2 × 15 ml spoons freshly chopped parsley	2 tablespoons freshly chopped parsley
salt	salt
freshly ground black pepper	freshly ground black pepper

Preparation time: 30 minutes, plus soaking
Cooking time: 25–30 minutes

Soak the mussels in cold water for about 1 hour. Drain the mussels and discard any which are open. Place the closed mussels in a large saucepan with the wine, water, onion and bouquet garni. Bring to the boil, cover with a tight-fitting lid and simmer for 10 minutes, shaking the pan frequently during this time. Drain and discard any mussels which have not opened. Remove the mussels from their shells.

Thread the mussels on to oiled long kebab skewers, alternating them with pieces of bacon and red and green pepper.

Put the softened butter in a bowl with the garlic, parsley, and salt and pepper to taste. Beat well to mix, then brush over the kebabs to cover them thickly.

Cook the kebabs on a rack under a preheated hot grill for 10–15 minutes until sizzling hot. Turn them frequently during this time, brushing and basting them with any remaining butter and the juices from the grill pan. Serve immediately.

Sole au whisky
Pan-fried sole with whisky sauce

Metric	Imperial
40 g butter	1½ oz butter
2 Dover or lemon sole, divided into 8 fillets and skinned	2 Dover or lemon sole, divided into 8 fillets and skinned
1 small fennel bulb (about 175 g), trimmed and thinly sliced	1 small fennel bulb (about 6 oz), trimmed and thinly sliced
1 garlic clove, peeled and crushed with 1 × 2.5 ml spoon salt	1 garlic clove, peeled and crushed with ½ teaspoon salt
4 × 15 ml spoons whisky	4 tablespoons whisky
100 g peeled prawns	4 oz peeled prawns
2 large firm tomatoes, skinned, seeded and chopped	2 large firm tomatoes, skinned, seeded and chopped
150 ml double cream	¼ pint double cream
salt	salt
freshly ground black pepper	freshly ground black pepper

Preparation time: 20 minutes
Cooking time: 25–35 minutes

For a special occasion main course, garnish with a few whole unpeeled prawns.

Melt 25 g/1 oz butter in a large non-stick frying pan. Add the sole in a single layer, 4 fillets at a time, and fry very gently for 2–3 minutes on each side until cooked through but not browned. Remove from the pan with a fish slice and keep hot in the lowest possible oven.

Melt the remaining butter in the pan, add the fennel and garlic and fry gently for about 5–10 minutes until the fennel has softened, stirring occasionally.

Increase the heat, add the whisky and stir until reduced slightly, then lower the heat and stir in the prawns and tomatoes. Simmer gently for 5 minutes, then stir in the cream. Heat through, then taste and adjust the seasoning.

To serve, arrange the sole on a warmed serving platter. Remove the prawns and tomato mixture from the pan with a slotted spoon and arrange on top of the fish. Pour over the remaining sauce and serve immediately.

Turbot au champagne
Turbot with sparkling white wine

Preparation time: 10–15 minutes
Cooking time: 35–40 minutes
Oven: 180°C, 350°F, Gas Mark 4

Metric	*Imperial*
50 g butter	*2 oz butter*
3 shallots or 1 medium onion, peeled and finely chopped	*3 shallots or 1 medium onion, peeled and finely chopped*
1 bunch watercress	*1 bunch watercress*
300 ml warm milk	*½ pint warm milk*
salt	*salt*
freshly ground black pepper	*freshly ground black pepper*
4 large fillets turbot, skinned	*4 large fillets turbot, skinned*
1 bay leaf	*1 bay leaf*
300 ml sparkling white wine	*½ pint sparkling white wine*

Brill or halibut can be used with equal success in this recipe; both are smaller and more economical fish, and more widely available than turbot. Although Champagne is used in cooking in France, sparkling white wine is a good substitute.

Melt the butter in a pan, add the shallots or onion and fry gently until soft. Reserve a few sprigs of watercress to garnish, finely chop the rest (stalks removed) and fry for a further 2 minutes, stirring constantly. Stir in the milk and salt and pepper to taste, bring to the boil, then lower the heat, cover and simmer gently for 15 minutes.

Meanwhile, place the fish in a single layer in a well-buttered ovenproof dish, sprinkle with salt and pepper and place the bay leaf on top. Pour in the wine, then cover with buttered foil and bake in a preheated oven for 10–15 minutes, or until the fish flakes easily with a fork.

Remove the fish with a slotted spoon, discarding the bay leaf, and place on a warmed serving platter. Cover with foil and keep hot.

Allow the milk and watercress mixture and the cooking liquid to cool slightly then purée in an electric blender. Taste and adjust the seasoning of the sauce, then drizzle a little over the fish on the serving platter. Pour the remaining sauce into a warmed sauceboat. Garnish the turbot with watercress sprigs and serve immediately, with the sauce handed separately.

Moules en brochette; Sole au whisky; Turbot au champagne

MEAT AND POULTRY

In France the choosing of meat, poultry and game is not a task to be taken lightly. To watch a French housewife buying meat in her local bouchier, charcuterie or market, to see her discuss the cut, size and cooking method with the shopkeeper or stallholder is evidence in itself. Meat is expensive in France, but at the same time it is of exceptionally high quality, and French butchers have a way of dividing a carcass that leaves the cook with very little wastage and a cut that both looks and tastes superb.

Tournedos de Dijon
Caramelized mustard steaks

Metric	*Imperial*
4 tournedos steaks, each weighing about 150 g	*4 tournedos steaks, each weighing about 5 oz*
freshly ground black pepper	*freshly ground black pepper*
6 × 15 ml spoons Dijon mustard	*6 tablespoons Dijon mustard*
50 g butter	*2 oz butter*
4 × 15 ml spoons demerara sugar	*4 tablespoons demerara sugar*
4 × 15 ml spoons brandy	*4 tablespoons brandy*
salt	*salt*

Preparation time: 5 minutes
Cooking time: 6–10 minutes

Tournedos steaks are so tender that they need very little cooking. They are usually sold tied with a strip of fat round them—snip the string and remove this fat before serving.

Sprinkle the steaks liberally on one side with pepper, then spread this side with one-third of the mustard. Melt the butter in a heavy-based frying pan and, when foaming, fry the steaks over brisk heat for 2 minutes, mustard side down. Spread the top side with half the remaining mustard, turn the steaks over and cook for a further 2 minutes for rare, 3 minutes for medium, and 4 minutes for well-done steaks.
Remove the steaks with a slotted spoon and place on a sheet of foil over the grill rack. Spread one side of each steak with the remaining mustard, then sprinkle with the sugar. Put under a preheated hot grill for about 2 minutes until caramelized and bubbling.
Meanwhile, heat the brandy gently in a small pan, remove from the heat and ignite. When the flames have subsided, pour the brandy into the steak juices in the frying pan. Stir vigorously, and add salt and pepper. Serve the steaks with the juices poured over.

Epaule d'agneau aux asperges
Lamb with asparagus sauce

Metric	*Imperial*
25 g butter	*1 oz butter*
1 medium onion, peeled and thinly sliced	*1 medium onion, peeled and thinly sliced*
1–2 garlic cloves, peeled and crushed with 1 × 2.5 spoon salt	*1–2 garlic cloves, peeled and crushed with ½ teaspoon salt*
1 kg boneless shoulder of lamb, trimmed of fat and cut into cubes	*2 lb boneless shoulder of lamb, trimmed of fat and cut into cubes*
juice of 1 lemon	*juice of 1 lemon*
300 ml chicken stock	*½ pint chicken stock*
freshly ground black pepper	*freshly ground black pepper*
1 × 225 g packet frozen asparagus spears, defrosted	*1 × 8 oz packet frozen asparagus spears, defrosted*
salt	*salt*
150 ml double cream, to finish	*¼ pint double cream, to finish*

Preparation time: 15 minutes
Cooking time: 2–2½ hours
Oven: 160°C, 325°F, Gas Mark 3

You will need a 2 kg/4 lb shoulder of lamb in order to have 1 kg/2 lb boneless meat. Ask the butcher to bone it for you as it can be a time-consuming task.

Melt the butter in a large flameproof casserole, add the onion and fry gently until soft. Add the garlic and lamb and fry over moderate heat until the lamb is lightly browned on all sides.
Stir the lemon juice into the pan, together with the stock and pepper to taste. Bring to the boil, then lower the heat and simmer gently for 5 minutes. Trim the tips off the asparagus spears and reserve. Stir the spears into the lamb mixture, then cover and transfer to a preheated oven. Cook for 1½–2 hours or until the lamb is tender, stirring occasionally. Meanwhile cook the reserved asparagus tips in simmering water for 3–5 minutes. Drain and set aside.
Return the casserole to the top of the stove and spoon away any fat from the surface. Taste and adjust the seasoning of the sauce. Mix together the cream and reserved asparagus tips, then pour carefully over the surface of the casserole in a thin, even layer. Heat through gently, without stirring, then serve.

Tournedos de Dijon; Epaule d'agneau aux asperges

Paupiettes de boeuf
Beef rolls with anchovy and capers

Preparation time: 40 minutes, plus soaking
Cooking time: 1–1¼ hours

Metric
4 thin slices rump
  steak, 100–175 g each
salt
freshly ground black
  pepper
2 × 15 ml spoons
  vegetable oil
4 rashers streaky bacon,
  rinds removed, chopped
3 shallots or 1 medium
  onion, peeled and
  finely chopped
300 ml full-bodied red
  wine
300 ml beef stock or
  water
1 bouquet garni

Stuffing:
1 × 50 g can anchovies,
  drained and soaked in
  milk for 20 minutes
100 g fresh white
  breadcrumbs
2 × 15 ml spoons capers,
  drained and crushed
2 shallots or 1 small
  onion, peeled and
  very finely chopped
2 × 15 ml spoons finely
  chopped parsley
finely grated rind and
  juice of 1 lemon
1 egg, beaten

To finish:
1 × 15 ml spoon softened
  butter
2 × 15 ml spoons plain
  flour

Imperial
4 thin slices rump
  steak, 4–6 oz each
salt
freshly ground black
  pepper
2 tablespoons vegetable
  oil
4 rashers streaky bacon,
  rinds removed, chopped
3 shallots or 1 medium
  onion, peeled and
  finely chopped
½ pint full-bodied red
  wine
½ pint beef stock or
  water
1 bouquet garni

Stuffing:
1 × 2 oz can anchovies,
  drained and soaked in
  milk for 20 minutes
4 oz fresh white
  breadcrumbs
2 tablespoons capers,
  drained and crushed
2 shallots or 1 small
  onion, peeled and
  very finely chopped
2 tablespoons finely
  chopped parsley
finely grated rind and
  juice of 1 lemon
1 egg, beaten

To finish:
1 tablespoon softened
  butter
2 tablespoons plain
  flour

For a more economical dish, use thin slices of silver-side. Ask your butcher to beat the silverside with a mallet to tenderize it, or do this yourself with a rolling pin. Allow an extra 15 minutes' cooking time.

To make the stuffing, drain the anchovies, pat dry with paper towels, then chop roughly. Mix the anchovies with the remaining stuffing ingredients and pepper to taste, adding a few drops of milk if the mixture seems dry.

Spread the slices of beef flat on a board or work surface and cut each lengthwise into two halves. Sprinkle with salt and pepper. Divide the stuffing equally between the 8 pieces of meat, placing it at one end and rolling the meat neatly round it. Tie with string or trussing thread and set aside.

Heat the oil in a flameproof casserole, add the bacon and fry over moderate heat until lightly browned. Lower the heat, add the shallots or onion and fry gently until soft. Remove with a slotted spoon and drain on paper towels.

Add the paupiettes and fry until browned on all sides. Add the bacon and onions and pour in the wine and stock. Tuck the bouquet garni amongst the paupiettes, then sprinkle lightly with salt and pepper. Cover and simmer gently for 45 minutes–1 hour until the beef is tender.

Remove the paupiettes with a slotted spoon and cut off the string or thread. Place on a warmed serving platter, cover with foil and keep warm.

To finish, work the butter and flour to a paste (beurre manié) in a small bowl. Remove the bouquet garni from the liquid in the pan. Add the beurre manié a little at a time, whisking vigorously over high heat until the sauce thickens. Taste and adjust the seasoning, then pour over the paupiettes. Serve immediately.

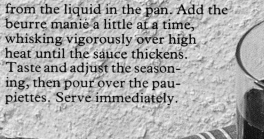

Boeuf au poivre vert
Beef with green peppercorns

Preparation time: 30 minutes
Cooking time: 2–2½ hours
Oven: 160°C, 325°F, Gas Mark 3

Metric
2 × 15 ml spoons
vegetable oil
1 kg chuck steak,
trimmed of excess
fat and cut into
large chunks
1 large onion, peeled
and chopped
2–3 celery sticks,
chopped
1 garlic clove, peeled
and crushed with 1 ×
2.5 ml spoon salt
4 rashers streaky bacon,
rinds removed, chopped
3 × 15 ml spoons green
peppercorns, drained
3 × 15 ml spoons freshly
chopped parsley
300 ml dry white wine
150 ml beef stock or
water
2 bay leaves
salt

Imperial
2 tablespoons vegetable
oil
2 lb chuck steak,
trimmed of excess
fat and cut into
large chunks
1 large onion, peeled
and chopped
2–3 celery sticks,
chopped
1 garlic clove, peeled
and crushed with ½
teaspoon salt
4 rashers streaky bacon,
rinds removed, chopped
3 tablespoons green
peppercorns, drained
3 tablespoons freshly
chopped parsley
½ pint dry white wine
¼ pint beef stock or
water
2 bay leaves
salt

Heat the oil in a large flameproof casserole, add the meat and fry over brisk heat until browned on all sides. Remove with a slotted spoon and drain on paper towels.

Lower the heat and add the onion, celery, garlic and bacon to the casserole. Fry gently until the vegetables are softened and the bacon lightly coloured, stirring constantly with a wooden spoon.

Crush 2 × 15 ml spoons/2 tablespoons peppercorns in a mortar and pestle, then stir into the casserole with 2 × 15 ml spoons/2 tablespoons parsley. Fry for 2–3 minutes, stirring, then return the beef to the casserole.

Stir in the wine and stock or water and bring to the boil. Add the bay leaves and salt to taste, then cover with a tight-fitting lid. Transfer to a preheated oven and cook for 1½–2 hours or until the beef is tender.

Remove from the oven and discard the bay leaves. Taste and adjust the seasoning, then sprinkle with the remaining peppercorns and parsley.

Left: Paupiettes de boeuf; Below: Boeuf au poivre vert

Filet de porc tourangeau
Pork with prunes and white wine

Metric
16 prunes
300 ml dry white wine
50 g butter
750 g pork fillet (tenderloin), cut into bite-sized pieces
salt
freshly ground black pepper
2 × 15 ml spoons redcurrant jelly
1 × 5 ml spoon lemon juice
150 ml double cream

Imperial
16 prunes
½ pint dry white wine
2 oz butter
1½ lb pork fillet (tenderloin), cut into bite-sized pieces
salt
freshly ground black pepper
2 tablespoons redcurrant jelly
1 teaspoon lemon juice
¼ pint double cream

Preparation time: 15 minutes, plus soaking
Cooking time: 50 minutes

Put the prunes in a shallow bowl, pour in the wine, cover and soak overnight.
Drain the prunes, reserving the liquid, and remove the stones.
Melt the butter in a flameproof casserole, add the pork and cook over brisk heat until lightly coloured on all sides. Sprinkle with salt and pepper. Add the prunes, pour over the reserved liquid and bring to the boil. Lower the heat, cover and simmer gently for 30 minutes or until the pork is tender.
Remove the pork and prunes from the pan with a slotted spoon and place on a warmed serving platter. Keep hot at the lowest possible setting in the oven.
Add the redcurrant jelly and lemon juice to the pan and stir until the jelly has melted. Stir in the cream and bring to the boil. Continue boiling for 5–10 minutes until the sauce is thickened and just beginning to turn golden, whisking continuously with a wire ballon whisk. Taste and adjust the seasoning, then pour over the pork. Serve immediately.

Porc au lait
Pork in milk

Metric	**Imperial**
1 × 1.5 kg loin of pork, skinned and boned	1 × 3 lb loin of pork, skinned and boned
2 × 15 ml spoons light Dijon mustard	2 tablespoons light Dijon mustard
4 garlic cloves, peeled and cut into thin slivers	4 garlic cloves, peeled and cut into thin slivers
salt	salt
freshly ground black pepper	freshly ground black pepper
50 g unsalted butter	2 oz unsalted butter
900 ml milk	1½ pints milk
150 ml double cream	¼ pint double cream

Preparation time: 15 minutes
Cooking time: 2 hours
Oven: 160°C, 325°F, Gas Mark 3

Ask your butcher to bone the pork for you and to cut away all the skin and most of the fat underneath the skin. If you make a slit horizontally through the centre of the joint before spreading with mustard, it will be much easier to roll the meat into a neat shape.

Place the meat on a board or work surface, fat side downward. Spread half the mustard over the meat, then dot with the slivers of garlic and sprinkle with salt and pepper. Roll the meat as neatly as possible, then tie with fine string or trussing thread.
Melt the butter in a flameproof casserole, add the pork and fry over moderate heat until lightly browned on all sides. Pour in the milk and bring to the boil, then lower the heat and sprinkle with salt and pepper. Cover the casserole and transfer to a preheated oven. Cook for 1½ hours or until the pork is tender, then remove from the casserole, discard the string and place on a warmed serving platter.
Strain the milk and cooking juices into a heavy-based pan and stir in the cream. Bring to the boil and continue boiling for 5–10 minutes until the sauce is thickened and just beginning to turn golden, whisking continuously with a wire balloon whisk. Remove from the heat, stir in the remaining mustard, taste and adjust the seasoning. Serve the pork cut into thin slices, with the sauce handed separately in a warmed sauceboat.

Porc en sanglier
Pork marinated in red wine

Metric	**Imperial**
1 × 1.5 kg leg of pork	1 × 3¼ lb leg of pork
40 g lard or butter	1½ oz lard or butter
2 × 15 ml spoons redcurrant jelly	2 tablespoons redcurrant jelly
Marinade:	**Marinade:**
300 ml red wine	½ pint red wine
1 carrot, peeled and sliced	1 carrot, peeled and sliced
1 onion, peeled and sliced	1 onion, peeled and sliced
2 celery sticks, chopped	2 celery sticks, chopped
1 × 15 ml spoon juniper berries, crushed	1 tablespoon juniper berries, crushed
2 garlic cloves, peeled and crushed with 1 × 2.5 ml spoon salt	2 garlic cloves, peeled and crushed with ½ teaspoon salt
2 bay leaves, halved	2 bay leaves, halved
1 bouquet garni	1 bouquet garni
freshly ground black pepper	freshly ground black pepper

Preparation time: about 30 minutes, plus marinating
Cooking time: about 2 hours
Oven: 160°C, 325°F, Gas Mark 3

Remove the rind and most of the fat from the pork and cut out the bone from the centre of the meat. The bone can be left, but it is easier to carve without it. Put the marinade ingredients in a large bowl. Add the pork, baste well, then cover tightly and marinate in the refrigerator for up to 3 days, turning the meat and basting frequently during this time.
Remove the pork from the marinade and pat thoroughly dry with paper towels. Tie the joint securely with string, as neatly as possible. Strain the marinade, reserving the vegetables and discarding the bouquet garni and bay leaves.
Melt the lard or butter in a large flameproof casserole, add the pork and fry briskly until browned on all sides. Remove and set aside. Lower the heat, and gently fry the reserved vegetables until lightly coloured.
Place the meat on top of the vegetables and pour over the reserved marinade. Cover with a tight-fitting lid and cook in a preheated oven for 1¾–2 hours, basting frequently.
Lift the pork out of the casserole, remove the string and place on a warmed serving platter. Keep warm. Transfer the casserole to the top of the stove and stir in the redcurrant jelly. Heat through until the jelly has melted. Taste and adjust the seasoning, then serve with the sauce in a warmed sauceboat.

Filet de porc tourangeau; Porc en sanglier; Porc au lait

Epaule d'agneau aux haricots
Lamb with haricot beans

Metric
3 garlic cloves, peeled
1 × 2 kg shoulder of
  lamb, boned, rolled
  and tied
salt
freshly ground black
  pepper
2 × 15 ml spoons olive
  oil
2 onions, peeled
225 g tomatoes, skinned,
  seeded and chopped
150 ml dry white wine
  or water
2 × 5 ml spoons freshly
  chopped rosemary or
  1 × 5 ml spoon dried
  rosemary
225 g dried haricot
  beans, soaked in cold
  water overnight
1 whole clove
1 carrot, peeled and
  quartered
1 bouquet garni

Imperial
3 garlic cloves, peeled
1 × 4½ lb shoulder of
  lamb, boned, rolled
  and tied
salt
freshly ground black
  pepper
2 tablespoons olive
  oil
2 onions, peeled
8 oz tomatoes, skinned,
  seeded and chopped
¼ pint dry white wine
  or water
2 teaspoons freshly
  chopped rosemary or
  1 teaspoon dried
  rosemary
8 oz dried haricot beans,
  soaked in cold water
  overnight
1 whole clove
1 carrot, peeled and
  quartered
1 bouquet garni

Preparation time: about 20 minutes, plus soaking
Cooking time: about 1¾–2¼ hours
Oven: 160°C, 325°F, Gas Mark 3

Ask your butcher to bone, roll and tie the lamb as this can be a time-consuming task to do yourself at home. Alternatively, a leg of lamb can be used.

Cut 2 garlic cloves into slivers. Make several incisions in the lamb with a sharp, pointed knife and insert the garlic slivers. Rub salt and pepper into the skin of the lamb.
Heat the oil in a large flameproof casserole, and brown the lamb on all sides over brisk heat. Lower the heat, remove from the pan and set aside.
Chop 1 onion, add to the pan and fry gently until soft and golden. Crush the remaining garlic clove with a little salt, then add to the onion with the tomatoes, wine or water, rosemary and pepper to taste. Bring to the boil, stirring, then lower the heat and return the lamb to the pan. Cover, transfer to a preheated oven and cook for 1½–2 hours or until the lamb is cooked to your liking.
Meanwhile, drain the beans and place in a pan. Stick the clove into the remaining whole onion, then add to the beans with the carrot and bouquet garni. Cover with fresh cold water and bring to the boil, then lower the heat, half cover with a lid and simmer for 1½–2 hours or until the beans are tender.
When the lamb is cooked, lift out of the casserole and remove the string. Place the lamb on a warmed serving platter and cover with foil. Turn the oven down to its lowest possible setting and place the lamb in the oven to keep warm.
Drain the beans, discarding the onion, carrot and bouquet garni. Stir the beans into the cooking liquid in the casserole and simmer on top of the stove for a few minutes. Taste and adjust the seasoning, then spoon around the lamb on the platter. Serve immediately.
Serves 4–6

Epaule d'agneau aux haricots; Gigot de mouton au genièvre

Gigot de mouton au genièvre
Roast leg of lamb with juniper

Metric
1 × 1.5 kg leg of lamb
4 garlic cloves, peeled
3 × 15 ml spoons juniper
  berries
salt
75 ml olive oil
3 × 15 ml spoons cider
  or wine vinegar
2 × 5 ml spoons freshly
  chopped rosemary
2 × 5 ml spoons freshly
  chopped marjoram
freshly ground black
  pepper

Imperial
1 × 3¼ lb leg of lamb
4 garlic cloves, peeled
3 tablespoons juniper
  berries
salt
3 fl oz olive oil
3 tablespoons cider or
  wine vinegar
2 teaspoons freshly
  chopped rosemary
2 teaspoons freshly
  chopped marjoram
freshly ground black
  pepper

Preparation time: 15 minutes, plus marinating
Cooking time: about 1½ hours
Oven: 190°C, 375°F, Gas Mark 5

The lamb is marinated in this recipe for up to 3 days and the longer you leave it to marinate, the better it will taste when cooked.

Cut deep incisions in the lamb with a sharp pointed knife, making as many as possible close to the bone. Into these incisions insert 2 garlic cloves cut into thin slivers, adding a juniper berry with each garlic sliver. Crush the remaining garlic and juniper berries in a mortar and pestle. Rub 1 × 5 ml spoon/1 teaspoon salt all over the surface of the lamb, then rub in the crushed garlic and juniper mixture.

Place the lamb in a large shallow dish. Mix the oil and vinegar in a small bowl with the herbs and pepper to taste. Brush all over the lamb. Cover and leave to marinate in the refrigerator for up to 3 days, turning the meat over and brushing it with the marinade as often as possible.

Place the lamb in a roasting tin, pour over the marinade from the dish, then roast in a preheated oven for 1½ hours or until the lamb is cooked to your liking. Turn the joint over frequently during the roasting time and baste with the marinade and cooking juices. Transfer the cooked joint to a warmed serving dish, then leave to stand in a warm place for 5 minutes before carving. Serve hot.

Variation:
In France the lamb would be served as it is, with only the juices from the roasting tin. If you prefer to serve a gravy, place the roasting tin on top of the stove after removing the lamb and stir in 2 × 15 ml spoons/2 tablespoons plain flour. Cook over moderate heat for 2 minutes until browned, stirring constantly, then gradually stir in 150 ml/¼ pint full-bodied red wine and 300 ml/½ pint water. Bring to the boil, then lower the heat and simmer gently for a few minutes until thickened. Add salt and pepper to taste, then pour into a warmed sauceboat.

Rognons au madère
Kidneys in Madeira

Metric
75 g butter
12 lamb's kidneys
   skinned and sliced,
   with cores removed
100 g button mushrooms,
   thinly sliced
salt
freshly ground black
   pepper
2 shallots or 1 small
   onion, peeled and
   finely chopped
1 garlic clove, peeled
   and crushed with
   1 × 2.5 ml salt
1 × 15 ml spoon plain
   flour
4 × 15 ml spoons Madeira
2 × 15 ml spoons freshly
   chopped parsley
2 × 15 ml spoons
   Moutarde de Meaux

Imperial
3 oz butter
12 lamb's kidneys
   skinned and sliced,
   with cores removed
4 oz button mushrooms,
   thinly sliced
salt
freshly ground black
   pepper
2 shallots or 1 small
   onion, peeled and
   finely chopped
1 garlic clove, peeled
   and crushed with
   ½ teaspoon salt
1 tablespoon plain
   flour
4 tablespoons Madeira
2 tablespoons freshly
   chopped parsley
2 tablespoons Moutarde
   de Meaux

Preparation time: 15 minutes
Cooking time: 35 minutes

If you do not have Madeira, and do not want to go to the expense of buying a bottle specially for this dish, use a dry or medium sherry instead.

Melt 50 g/2 oz butter in a large heavy frying pan. Add the kidneys and mushrooms with salt and pepper and fry over moderate heat for about 8 minutes, shaking the pan constantly until the kidneys are lightly browned on all sides and the juices run faintly pink. Remove the kidneys and mushrooms from the pan with a slotted spoon and keep warm in the lowest possible oven. Pour the cooking juices into a jug.
Melt the remaining butter in the pan, add the shallots or onion and garlic and fry gently until soft and lightly coloured. Sprinkle in the flour and fry for a further 1–2 minutes, stirring constantly, then gradually add the Madeira and the reserved cooking juices. Bring to the boil, then lower the heat and return the kidneys and mushrooms to the pan. Stir to coat them in the sauce, then lower the heat and simmer very gently for 15 minutes until the kidneys are tender. Remove from the heat and stir in the parsley and mustard. Taste and adjust the seasoning, then transfer to a warmed serving dish. Serve immediately.

Estouffat de boeuf
Brisket of beef with red wine

Metric

2 × 15 ml spoons beef
  dripping or vegetable
  oil
1–1.125 kg joint brisket
  of beef
1 large onion, peeled
  and chopped
1 garlic clove, peeled
  and crushed with
  1 × 2.5 ml spoon salt
2 large carrots, peeled
  and sliced
2 leeks, sliced
300 ml full-bodied red
  wine
300 ml beef stock or
  water
1 bouquet garni
1 × 1.25 ml spoon ground
  cinnamon
1 × 1.25 ml spoon ground
  allspice
salt
freshly ground black
  pepper

To finish:

1 × 15 ml spoon
  Armagnac or brandy
  (optional)
1 × 15 ml spoon softened
  butter
2 × 15 ml spoons plain
  flour

Imperial

2 tablespoons beef
  dripping or vegetable
  oil
2–2½ lb joint brisket of
  beef
1 large onion, peeled
  and chopped
1 garlic clove, peeled
  and crushed with
  ½ teaspoon salt
2 large carrots, peeled
  and sliced
2 leeks, sliced
½ pint full-bodied red
  wine
½ pint beef stock or
  water
1 bouquet garni
¼ teaspoon ground
  cinnamon
¼ teaspoon ground
  allspice
salt
freshly ground black
  pepper

To finish:

1 tablespoon
  Armagnac or brandy
  (optional)
1 tablespoon softened
  butter
2 tablespoons plain
  flour

Preparation time: about 30 minutes
Cooking time: about 3½ hours
Oven: 150°C, 300°F, Gas Mark 2

Melt the dripping or oil in a large flameproof casserole, add the beef and fry over brisk heart until browned on all sides. Remove from the pan and set aside.

Lower the heat, add the onion and garlic to the pan and fry gently until soft. Add the carrots and leeks and fry for a further few minutes, stirring until lightly coloured.

Stir in the wine and stock or water and bring to the boil. Lower the heat, add the bouquet garni, cinnamon, allspice and salt and pepper to taste, then return the beef to the pan. Cover and transfer to a preheated oven and cook for 3 hours or until the beef is tender, basting occasionally.

Remove the beef from the pan and remove any strings or threads. Place the beef on a warmed serving platter. Warm the Armagnac gently in a small pan, remove from the heat and ignite. When the flames have subsided, pour the brandy over the beef. Keep the meat warm.

Work the butter and flour to a paste (beurre manié) in a small bowl. Remove the bouquet garni from the liquid in the pan. Add the beurre manié a little at a time, whisking vigorously over high heat until the sauce boils and thickens. Taste and adjust the seasoning, then pour a little sauce over the beef. Pour the remaining sauce into a warmed sauceboat.

Rognons au madère; Estouffat de boeuf

Sauté de veau au vermouth
Veal with vermouth and orange

Metric
4 veal escalopes, weighing
  about 100 g each
2 × 15 ml spoons plain
  flour
salt
freshly ground black
  pepper
50 g butter
2 × 15 ml spoons olive
  oil
juice of 2 oranges
150 ml dry white
  vermouth
2 × 5 ml spoons dark
  soft brown sugar
1–2 oranges, skinned
  and thinly sliced in
  rings

Imperial
4 veal escalopes, weighing
  about 4 oz each
2 tablespoons plain
  flour
salt
freshly ground black
  pepper
2 oz butter
2 tablespoons olive
  oil
juice of 2 oranges
$\frac{1}{4}$ pint dry white
  vermouth
2 teaspoons dark soft
  brown sugar
1–2 oranges, skinned
  and thinly sliced in
  rings

Preparation time: 10 minutes
Cooking time: about 25 minutes

For this dish the escalopes should be sliced very thin.

Beat the escalopes with a mallet or rolling pin. Pat them dry with paper towels, then coat evenly in the flour seasoned with salt and pepper. Melt 25 g/1 oz butter with the oil in a large heavy-based frying pan. Add the escalopes and fry over moderate heat for about 3 minutes on each side until lightly browned. Measure the orange juice and make up to 150 ml/$\frac{1}{4}$ pint with water, if necessary. Pour over the escalopes, then simmer gently for about 8 minutes or until the veal is tender, turning it over once during this time. Remove the veal from the pan with a slotted spoon, arrange on a warmed serving platter and keep hot in a very low oven. Pour the vermouth into the pan, stir in the sugar and increase the heat. Boil vigorously until the sauce has thickened and reduced, stirring continuously with a wooden spoon to loosen any sediment from the bottom and sides of the pan.
Remove the pan from the heat, stir in the remaining butter in pieces, then whisk until the butter has dissolved and the sauce has a shiny glaze. Taste and adjust the seasoning, then pour over the veal. Garnish with orange rings and serve immediately.

Sauté de veau au vermouth; Sauté de veau marengo

Sauté de veau marengo
Sautéed veal with mushrooms

Metric	Imperial
4 × 15 ml spoons olive oil	*4 tablespoons olive oil*
1 kg pie or stewing veal, cut into bite-sized pieces	*2 lb pie or stewing veal, cut into bite-sized pieces*
1 medium onion, peeled and finely chopped	*1 medium onion, peeled and finely chopped*
2 garlic cloves, peeled and crushed with 1 × 2.5 ml spoon salt	*2 garlic cloves, peeled and crushed with ½ teaspoon salt*
2 × 15 ml spoons plain flour	*2 tablespoons plain flour*
225 g tomatoes, skinned, seeded and chopped	*8 oz tomatoes, skinned, seeded and chopped*
300 ml dry white wine	*½ pint dry white wine*
150–300 ml chicken stock or water	*¼–½ pint chicken stock or water*
1 bouquet garni	*1 bouquet garni*
1 strip of orange peel	*1 strip of orange peel*
salt	*salt*
freshly ground black pepper	*freshly ground black pepper*
12 small pickling onions, peeled	*12 small pickling onions, peeled*
12 small button mushrooms	*12 small button mushrooms*
freshly chopped parsley, to garnish	*freshly chopped parsley, to garnish*

Preparation time: 30 minutes
Cooking time: about 2 hours

Heat 3 × 15 ml spoons/3 tablespoons oil in a large flameproof casserole, add the veal and fry over brisk heat until browned on all sides. Remove from the pan with a slotted spoon and set aside.

Lower the heat, add the chopped onion and garlic to the pan and fry gently until soft. Stir in the flour and fry for a further 2 minutes, stirring constantly. Stir in the tomatoes and fry for about 5 minutes, crushing them into the onion and garlic with a wooden spoon.

Return the veal to the pan and stir in the wine and 150 ml/¼ pint stock or water. Bring to the boil, then add the bouquet garni, orange peel and salt and pepper. Lower the heat, cover the pan and simmer gently for 1 hour or until the veal is barely tender, stirring occasionally.

Meanwhile, heat the remaining oil in a separate pan, add the whole onions and fry gently until lightly coloured on all sides. Add the mushrooms and fry for a further 2 minutes, then remove both onions and mushrooms from the pan with a slotted spoon and drain on paper towels.

Remove the veal from the casserole with a slotted spoon and set aside. Pass the cooking liquid through a sieve, pressing firmly to extract all the juices. Return the veal and sieved cooking juices to the rinsed-out casserole, then stir in the small onions and mushrooms. Stir in more stock or water if the sauce seems too thick.

Return the casserole to the heat, bring to the boil, then lower the heat and simmer gently for a further 30 minutes or until the veal is tender. Taste and adjust the seasoning of the sauce, then sprinkle liberally with chopped parsley.

Poulet à l'estragon
Chicken with tarragon butter sauce

Metric	Imperial
100 g butter	4 oz butter
1 × 2 kg oven-ready chicken	1 × 4 lb oven-ready chicken
4 garlic cloves, peeled	4 garlic cloves, peeled
2 × 15 ml spoons freshly chopped tarragon or 1 × 15 ml spoon dried tarragon	2 tablespoons freshly chopped tarragon or 1 tablespoon dried tarragon
salt	salt
freshly ground black pepper	freshly ground black pepper
2 × 15 ml spoons plain flour	2 tablespoons plain flour
450 ml dry white wine and water, mixed	¾ pint dry white wine and water, mixed

Preparation time: 10 minutes
Cooking time: 1 hour 40 minutes
Oven: 190°C, 375°F, Gas Mark 5

Use as much white wine as you can spare for the sauce, and for a dinner party main course swirl in 150 ml/¼ pint double cream just before serving. For an economical meal, the sauce can be made with chicken stock rather than the mixture of white wine and water.

Put half the butter inside the cavity of the chicken with 2 whole garlic cloves, half the tarragon and salt and pepper to taste. Truss with thread or fine string, then put in a roasting tin.
Crush the remaining garlic cloves with 1 × 2.5 ml spoon/½ teaspoon salt. Beat into the remaining butter with the rest of the tarragon until soft, then spread the mixture all over the skin of the chicken. Sprinkle with salt and pepper.
Roast in a preheated oven for about 1½ hours or until the juices of the chicken run clear when the thickest part of the thigh is pierced with a skewer. Turn the chicken over a quarter turn every 15 minutes during roasting, and baste with the cooking juices.
Transfer the chicken to a warmed serving platter and keep hot in the lowest possible oven. Pour off all but 2 × 15 ml spoons/2 tablespoons of the excess fat and juices from the roasting tin. Place the roasting tin on top of the stove over moderate heat and sprinkle in the flour. Cook for 1–2 minutes until golden brown, stirring constantly, then gradually stir in the wine and water mixture. Bring to the boil, then lower the heat and simmer until thickened, stirring all the time. Taste and adjust the seasoning, then pour into a warmed sauceboat. Serve the chicken immediately, with the sauce handed separately.

Poulet basquaise
Chicken Basque-style

Metric	Imperial
4 × 15 ml spoons olive oil	4 tablespoons olive oil
4 chicken portions, skinned	4 chicken portions, skinned
1 medium onion, peeled and finely chopped	1 medium onion, peeled and finely chopped
1 garlic clove, peeled and crushed with 1 × 2.5 ml spoon salt	1 garlic clove, peeled and crushed with ½ teaspoon salt
½ red pepper, cored, seeded and finely chopped	½ red pepper, cored, seeded and finely chopped
½ green pepper, cored, seeded and finely chopped	½ green pepper, cored, seeded and finely chopped
350 g tomatoes, skinned, seeded and chopped	12 oz tomatoes, skinned, seeded and chopped
150 ml chicken stock	¼ pint chicken stock
4 × 15 ml spoons brandy or medium sherry	4 tablespoons brandy or medium sherry
2 × 5 ml spoons freshly chopped rosemary or 1 × 5 ml spoon dried rosemary	2 teaspoons freshly chopped rosemary or 1 teaspoon dried rosemary
2 × 5 ml spoons freshly chopped thyme or 1 × 5 ml spoon dried thyme	2 teaspoons freshly chopped thyme or 1 teaspoon dried thyme
salt	salt
freshly ground black pepper	freshly ground black pepper

Preparation time: 30 minutes
Cooking time: about 1¼ hours

In the south-western corner of France, customs and cuisine are very closely linked with the Basque country across the border in Spain and onions, garlic, peppers and tomatoes are dominant features.

Heat the oil in a large flameproof casserole, add the chicken and fry gently until browned on all sides. Remove from the pan and set aside.
Add the onion to the pan and fry gently until soft. Add the garlic and peppers and fry for a further few minutes, then stir in the tomatoes, chicken stock or water and brandy and bring to the boil.
Lower the heat, add the rosemary, thyme, and salt and pepper to taste, then return the chicken to the pan. Simmer gently, uncovered, for 45 minutes or until the chicken is tender and the liquid and vegetables are reduced. Serve immediately.

Top: Poulet à l'estragon; Below: Poulet basquaise

Poulet au foie gras
Chicken with foie gras sauce

Metric	Imperial
4 chicken breasts, boned and skinned	4 chicken breasts, boned and skinned
1 garlic clove, peeled and halved	1 garlic clove, peeled and halved
50 g butter	2 oz butter
2 × 15 ml spoons olive oil	2 tablespoons olive oil
salt	salt
freshly ground black pepper	freshly ground black pepper
150 ml full-bodied red wine	¼ pint full-bodied red wine
1 × 150 g can pâté de foie gras	1 × 5 oz can pâté de foie gras
150 ml single cream	¼ pint single cream
175–225 g button mushrooms, finely sliced	6–8 oz button mushrooms, finely sliced

Preparation time: about 20 minutes
Cooking time: 45 minutes

Rub the chicken all over with the cut surfaces of the garlic. Melt half the butter with the oil in a large frying pan. Add the chicken and fry over moderate heat until golden on all sides. Sprinkle with salt and pepper to taste, pour in the wine and bring to the boil. Lower the heat, cover and cook gently for about 30 minutes or until the chicken is tender.

Meanwhile, put the pâté in a bowl and beat until smooth with a wooden spoon or electric beater. Gradually beat in the cream.

Remove the chicken from the pan with a slotted spoon and keep warm on a serving platter in the lowest possible oven. Stir the pâté mixture into the cooking juices in the pan a little at a time, whisking vigorously until a smooth sauce is formed. Add salt and pepper to taste, if necessary, then simmer gently for 5 minutes, stirring occasionally.

Meanwhile, melt the remaining butter in a separate pan. Add the mushrooms and fry over brisk heat for 1–2 minutes, shaking the pan constantly.

Pour the sauce over the chicken and garnish each portion with a cluster of mushroom slices. Serve immediately.

Poulet au fromage
Chicken with cheese and wine sauce

Metric	Imperial
4 chicken portions, skinned	4 chicken portions, skinned
1 × 15 ml spoon lemon juice	1 tablespoon lemon juice
salt	salt
freshly ground black pepper	freshly ground black pepper
75 g butter	3 oz butter
50 g plain flour	2 oz plain flour
150 ml dry white wine	¼ pint dry white wine
200 ml milk	⅓ pint milk
100 g Gruyère cheese, grated	4 oz Gruyère cheese, grated
1 × 1.25 ml spoon ground mace	¼ teaspoon ground mace
100 g button mushrooms, thinly sliced	4 oz button mushrooms, thinly sliced

Preparation time: 10–15 minutes
Cooking time: 50 minutes–1 hour 5 minutes
Oven: 180°C, 350°F, Gas Mark 4

Put the chicken portions in a single layer in a shallow flameproof casserole. Sprinkle over the lemon juice, and salt and pepper to taste, then dot with 25 g/1 oz butter. Cover with foil and cook in a preheated oven for 45 minutes to 1 hour until the chicken is just tender. Baste occasionally with the cooking juices during this time.

Fifteen minutes before the end of the cooking time, make the sauce. Melt the remaining butter in a heavy-based pan, add the flour and stir over low heat for 1–2 minutes. Remove from the heat and gradually add the wine and then the milk, beating with a wire balloon whisk after each addition. Return to the heat and bring to the boil, stirring constantly, then lower the heat and simmer until thick and smooth. Add 75 g/3 oz cheese, the mace, and salt and pepper to taste, and stir until the cheese has melted. Remove from the heat and stir in the mushrooms.

When the chicken is tender, drain off the cooking juices and stir into the cheese sauce. Pour the sauce over the chicken and sprinkle with the remaining cheese. Put under a preheated hot grill for 5 minutes until the cheese is melted and bubbling.

Clockwise from top: Poulet au foie gras; Lapin à la moutarde; Poulet au fromage

Lapin à la moutarde
Rabbit smothered in mustard

Metric	Imperial
4 rabbit portions (total weight about 1 kg)	4 rabbit portions (total weight about 2 lb)
6 × 15 ml spoons light Dijon mustard	6 tablespoons light Dijon mustard
4 × 15 ml spoons oil	4 tablespoons oil
225 g shallots or 2 medium onions, peeled and finely chopped	8 oz shallots or 2 medium onions, peeled and finely chopped
3 × 15 ml spoons plain flour	3 tablespoons plain flour
1 × 5 ml spoon freshly chopped rosemary or 1 × 2.5 ml spoon dried rosemary	1 teaspoon freshly chopped rosemary or ½ teaspoon dried rosemary
1 × 5 ml spoon freshly chopped thyme or 1 × 2.5 ml spoon dried thyme	1 teaspoon freshly chopped thyme or ½ teaspoon dried thyme
300 ml dry white wine or cider	½ pint dry white wine or cider
salt	salt
freshly ground black pepper	freshly ground black pepper
1 bunch watercress, to garnish	1 bunch watercress, to garnish

Preparation time: 15 minutes, plus marinating
Cooking time: 1¼–1½ hours

The quantity of mustard in this recipe can be adjusted to suit individual tastes, although it should be quite strong to be authentic.

Spread the rabbit with 4 × 15 ml spoons/4 tablespoons mustard, then cover and leave in a cool place for at least 4 hours, preferably overnight.

Heat the oil in a large flameproof casserole, add the rabbit pieces and fry over moderate heat until browned on all sides. Remove from the pan with a slotted spoon and set aside.

Add the shallots or onions to the pan and fry gently until soft. Stir in the flour, rosemary and thyme and fry for a further 1–2 minutes, stirring constantly. Stir in the wine or cider, bring to just below boiling point, then return the rabbit to the pan. Add salt and pepper to taste, cover and simmer gently for 45 minutes–1 hour or until the rabbit is tender.

Remove the rabbit from the sauce with a slotted spoon. Place in a warmed serving dish and keep hot. Stir in the remaining mustard, heat through, then taste and adjust the seasoning. Spoon the sauce over the rabbit pieces and garnish with watercress sprigs. Serve immediately.

Perdreaux aux raisins
Partridge with green grape sauce

Metric	Imperial
50 g butter	2 oz butter
2 partridges	2 partridges
salt	salt
freshly ground black pepper	freshly ground black pepper
2–3 celery sticks, finely chopped	2–3 celery sticks, finely chopped
2 shallots or 1 small onion, peeled and finely chopped	2 shallots or 1 small onion, peeled and finely chopped
225 g seedless green grapes, stalks removed	8 oz seedless green grapes, stalks removed
2 × 15 ml spoons brandy (optional)	2 tablespoons brandy (optional)
300 ml dry white wine	½ pint dry white wine

To finish:

Metric	Imperial
1 × 15 ml spoon softened butter	1 tablespoon softened butter
1 × 15 ml spoon plain flour	1 tablespoon plain flour

Preparation time: 15 minutes
Cooking time: about 1¼–1½ hours

In France partridges are immensely popular birds for the table although their season is confined to September to January. Oven-ready partridges are available fresh from butchers specializing in game. However, excellent-quality frozen birds are available from large supermarkets all year round. Defrost them for 24 hours in the refrigerator before cooking.

Cut half the butter into 2 equal pieces and place 1 piece inside each partridge. Sprinkle inside and out with salt and pepper.
Melt the remaining butter in a large flameproof casserole, add the partridges and fry over moderate heat until lightly browned on all sides. Remove and drain on paper towels.
Add the celery and shallots or onion to the casserole and fry gently until softened. Stir in the grapes and fry gently for a further 1–2 minutes, then place the partridges on top of the grapes.
If using the brandy, warm it gently in a small pan, remove from the heat and ignite. When the flames have subsided, pour the brandy over the partridges.
Pour the wine into the casserole and bring to boil. Lower the heat, add salt and pepper to taste, then cover and simmer gently for 45 minutes–1 hour until the partridges are tender when pierced with a skewer. Baste the partridges occasionally with the cooking liquid during this time.
Remove the partridges and discard the barding fat and trussing strings. Place the birds on a warmed serving platter, cover with foil and keep warm.
To finish, work the butter and flour to a paste (beurre manié). Add to the sauce in the pan a little at a time, whisking vigorously over high heat until the sauce thickens. Taste and adjust the seasoning, then pour a little sauce over each partridge breast. Serve with the remaining sauce in a warmed sauceboat.

Perdreaux aux raisins;
Canard aux cerises à l'aigre-doux

Canard aux cerises à l'aigre-doux
Duck with sweet and sour cherries

Metric	Imperial
1 × 2–2.25 kg duck	*1 × 4½–5 lb duck*
salt	*salt*
freshly ground black pepper	*freshly ground black pepper*
2 oranges	*2 oranges*
1 onion, peeled and quartered	*1 onion, peeled and quartered*
1 bouquet garni	*1 bouquet garni*
25 g butter, softened	*1 oz butter, softened*
1 × 425 g can sweetened red or black cherries	*1 × 15 oz can sweetened red or black cherries*
3 × 15 ml spoons red wine vinegar	*3 tablespoons red wine vinegar*
finely grated rind and juice of 1 orange	*finely grated rind and juice of 1 orange*
2 × 15 ml spoons cherry brandy (optional)	*2 tablespoons cherry brandy (optional)*
1 × 15 ml spoon arrowroot	*1 tablespoon arrowroot*

Preparation time: 15 minutes
Cooking time: about 2¼ hours
Oven: 220°C, 425°F, Gas Mark 7;
   180°C, 350°F, Gas Mark 4

Sprinkle the inside of the duck with salt and pepper. Cut 1 orange into quarters, then place inside the duck with the onion quarters and the bouquet garni. Truss with thread or fine string.

Place the duck on a rack in a roasting tin and prick the fattiest parts of the skin with the point of a fine skewer. Spread the softened butter all over the bird, then sprinkle with salt and pepper and the juice of the remaining orange.

Cover the duck with foil and roast in a preheated oven for 30 minutes. Reduce the oven temperature and roast for a further 1¾ hours or until the duck is tender and the juices run clear when the thickest part of the thigh is pierced with a skewer. Remove the foil for the last 30 minutes of the cooking time so that the skin becomes crisp and golden brown, sprinkling with more salt if necessary.

During the last 15 minutes of the cooking time, make the sauce. Drain the cherries, reserving half the juice from the can. Put the cherry juice, wine vinegar, orange rind and juice in a measuring jug with the cherry brandy, if using. Make up to 450 ml/¾ pint with water.

In a separate jug, mix the arrowroot to a paste with a little of the measured liquid. Pour the remaining measured liquid into a pan and bring to the boil. Stir in the arrowroot paste and boil vigorously until the sauce thickens. Lower the heat, add the cherries and salt and pepper to taste, then simmer gently for 2–3 minutes until the cherries are heated through.

Remove the thread or string from the duck and place on a warmed serving platter. Pour a little of the sauce over the breast. Serve with the remaining sauce in a warmed sauceboat.

Serves 3–4

VEGETABLES

The vegetable in France holds an exalted place in culinary terms. Rarely will you be served a vegetable on the same plate as the main course, for the French like to savour their vegetables on their own, after the main course. This is why such a great deal of care and attention goes into their selection, preparation and cooking. Usually only one (or at the most two) vegetables are served during the main meal of the day, plus one of the many different potato dishes. Fresh vegetables are always preferred to frozen and canned, and the younger and fresher they are the better, because they are almost always cooked for the shortest possible time, in the minimum amount of liquid.

Fèves à la saucisse à l'ail; Artichauts farcis parisiens

Fèves à la saucisse à l'ail
Broad beans with garlic sausage

Metric	Imperial
1¾ kg fresh broad beans, shelled, or 450 g frozen broad beans	4 lb fresh broad beans, shelled, or 1 lb frozen broad beans
salt	salt
25 g butter	1 oz butter
2 shallots or 1 onion, peeled and finely chopped	2 shallots or 1 onion, peeled and finely chopped
100 g piece garlic sausage, roughly chopped	4 oz piece garlic sausage, roughly chopped
2 × 5 ml spoons freshly chopped savory or 1 × 5 ml spoon dried savory	2 teaspoons freshly chopped savory or 1 teaspoon dried savory
freshly ground black pepper	freshly ground black pepper
150 ml single cream	¼ pint single cream

Preparation time: 5–10 minutes
Cooking time: 20–25 minutes for fresh beans;
            10–15 minutes for frozen

Cook the beans in boiling salted water, allowing 15–20 minutes for fresh beans, 6–8 minutes for frozen or according to packet instruction.
Meanwhile, melt the butter in a heavy-based pan, add the shallots or onion and fry gently until soft and lightly coloured. Add the garlic sausage and fry for 2–3 minutes, stirring frequently.
Drain the beans and add to the onion and garlic sausage with the savory, and salt and pepper to taste. Fold the ingredients together well, then stir in the cream and heat through gently without boiling. Transfer to a warmed serving dish and serve immediately. Serve with lamb or pork dishes, especially grilled or roasted meat.

Artichauts farcis parisiens
Braised stuffed artichokes

Preparation time: about 40 minutes
Cooking time: about 1 hour
Oven: 180°C, 350°F, Gas Mark 4

Metric
4 young globe artichokes
½ lemon
1 × 15 ml spoon lemon
   juice
2 × 15 ml spoons olive oil
1 medium onion, peeled
   and chopped
2 carrots, peeled and very
   thinly sliced
salt
freshly ground black
   pepper
25 g butter
300 ml dry white wine

Stuffing:
50 g unsalted butter
50 g button mushrooms,
   finely chopped
50 g fresh white
   breadcrumbs
2 × 15 ml spoons freshly
   chopped parsley
2 × 5 ml spoons freshly
   chopped thyme or 1 × 5
   ml spoon dried thyme
2 garlic cloves, peeled
   and crushed with 1 ×
   2.5 ml spoon salt
finely grated rind of 1
   lemon

Imperial
4 young globe artichokes
½ lemon
1 tablespoon lemon
   juice
2 tablespoons olive oil
1 medium onion, peeled
   and chopped
2 carrots, peeled and very
   thinly sliced
salt
freshly ground black
   pepper
1 oz butter
½ pint dry white wine

Stuffing:
2 oz unsalted butter
2 oz button mushrooms,
   finely chopped
2 oz fresh white
   breadcrumbs
2 tablespoons freshly
   chopped parsley
2 teaspoons freshly
   chopped thyme or 1
   teaspoon dried thyme
2 garlic cloves, peeled
   and crushed with ½
   teaspoon salt
finely grated rind of 1
   lemon

Serve this substantial vegetable dish as an accompaniment to plain roast or grilled meat, or on its own as a starter before a light main course.

Cut the stems off the artichokes and level the bases so that they will stand upright. Remove the tough outer leaves, then cut off the tops of the remaining leaves about one-third of the way down to expose the chokes in the centre. Rub the cut surfaces immediately with the cut lemon to prevent them discolouring.

Plunge the artichokes into a pan of boiling water to which the lemon juice has been added. Bring back to the boil, then lower the heat and simmer for 10 minutes. Remove the artichokes from the pan with a slotted spoon, then stand them upside down in a colander to drain.

Meanwhile, make the stuffing. Melt the butter in a pan, add the mushrooms and fry gently for 2–3 minutes. Transfer to a bowl with the cooking juices and add all the remaining stuffing ingredients with salt and pepper to taste. Mix together well.

Stand the artichokes the right way up and carefully remove the chokes from their centres with a sharp-edged teaspoon. Fill the cavities with the stuffing.

Heat the oil in a large flameproof casserole into which the artichokes will just fit. Add the onion and carrots with salt and pepper to taste, and fry gently until lightly coloured. Stand the artichokes in the casserole, dot the top of each one with butter, then pour the wine around them and bring slowly to the boil.

Cover the casserole with a lid and transfer to a preheated oven. Cook for about 40 minutes or until the artichokes are tender. Serve immediately.

Tomates niçoises
Tomatoes with basil and cream

Metric	Imperial
3 × 15 ml spoons olive oil	3 tablespoons olive oil
1 large onion, peeled and thinly sliced	1 large onion, peeled and thinly sliced
10 large tomatoes, skinned and thinly sliced	10 large tomatoes, skinned and thinly sliced
2 × 5 ml spoons sugar	2 teaspoons sugar
1 × 15 ml spoon freshly chopped parsley	1 tablespoon freshly chopped parsley
2 × 5 ml spoons freshly chopped basil or 1 × 5 ml spoon dried basil	2 teaspoons freshly chopped basil or 1 teaspoon dried basil
salt	salt
freshly ground black pepper	freshly ground black pepper
300 ml double cream	½ pint double cream
75 g fresh white breadcrumbs	3 oz fresh white breadcrumbs
25 g butter	1 oz butter

Preparation time: 30 minutes
Cooking time: 45–50 minutes
Oven: 180°C, 350°F, Gas Mark 4

Heat 2 × 15 ml spoons/2 tablespoons oil in a frying pan, and fry the onion slices gently until soft.
Brush a baking dish with the remaining oil. Put one-third of the tomato slices in the bottom of the dish, sprinkle with a little sugar, parsley and basil, and salt and pepper to taste. Top with a few onion slices, then pour in about one-third of the cream.
Repeat these layers twice more, then sprinkle over the breadcrumbs to cover the cream completely. Dot with the butter. Bake, uncovered, in a preheated oven for 35–40 minutes, until golden.

Aubergines à l'ail
Aubergines roasted with garlic

Metric	Imperial
4 medium aubergines (175–225 g each), tops removed	4 medium aubergines (6–8 oz each), tops removed
6 × 15 ml spoons olive oil	6 tablespoons olive oil
4 garlic cloves, peeled and cut into thin slivers	4 garlic cloves, peeled and cut into thin slivers
4 tomatoes, skinned and thinly sliced	4 tomatoes, skinned and thinly sliced
4 × 5 ml spoons freshly chopped basil or 2 × 5 ml spoons dried basil	4 teaspoons freshly chopped basil or 2 teaspoons dried basil
salt	salt
freshly ground black pepper	freshly ground black pepper
150 ml dry white wine or water	¼ pint dry white wine or water

Preparation time: 20 minutes
Cooking time: 1½ hours
Oven: 180°C, 350°F, Gas Mark 4

Make 4 deep lengthways incisions in each aubergine with a sharp knife. Brush 1 × 15 ml spoon/1 tablespoon olive oil over the cut flesh of each aubergine, then insert the garlic slivers in them, allowing 1 garlic clove for each aubergine. Insert the tomato slices into the incisions on top of the garlic, then sprinkle in the basil, and salt and pepper to taste.
Stand the aubergines in a single layer in a baking dish into which they just fit. Pour the wine into the bottom of the dish, drizzle the remaining oil over the top, and sprinkle with more salt and pepper.
Cover with foil, then bake in a preheated oven for 1½ hours or until the aubergines are tender.
Serve with any roast or grilled meat.

Pommes de terre soufflées
Souffléed baked potatoes

Metric
4 large potatoes
1 medium cooking apple
50 g unsalted butter,
   softened
2 eggs, separated
1 × 5 ml spoon dried sage
salt
freshly ground black
   pepper

Imperial
4 large potatoes
1 medium cooking apple
2 oz unsalted butter,
   softened
2 eggs, separated
1 teaspoon dried sage
salt
freshly ground black
   pepper

Preparation time: about 40 minutes
Cooking time: 1¼–1¾ hours
Oven: 200°C, 400°F, Gas Mark 6

Prick the potatoes all over with a fine skewer, then place directly on the shelf of a preheated oven. Bake for 1–1½ hours or until the potatoes are soft and tender when gently squeezed between your fingers.

Remove the potatoes from the oven and slice each one in half lengthways. Scoop out the flesh into a bowl and mash well. Reserve the skins.

Peel, core and grate the apple, then beat into the potato flesh with the butter, egg yolks, sage and salt and pepper to taste.

In a separate bowl, beat the egg whites until stiff, then fold into the potato mixture. Spoon the mixture into the reserved potato skins, dividing it equally and moulding it into a domed shape. Return to the oven, on a shelf above the centre, and bake for a further 15 minutes or until puffed up and golden brown. Serve with casseroles, barbecued meat or with cold meats and a salad.

Beignets de pommes de terre
Potato fritters with cream cheese

Metric
1 kg potatoes, peeled
100 g cream cheese
2 eggs
2 × 15 ml spoons snipped
   chives or freshly
   chopped parsley
salt
freshly ground black
   pepper
vegetable oil, for shallow
   frying

Imperial
2 lb potatoes, peeled
4 oz cream cheese
2 eggs
2 tablespoons snipped
   chives or freshly
   chopped parsley
salt
freshly ground black
   pepper
vegetable oil, for shallow
   frying

Preparation time: about 30 minutes
Cooking time: about 15–20 minutes

Grate the potatoes, squeeze them in your hands to extract as much moisture as possible, then pat dry with paper towels.

Put the cream cheese in a bowl and beat until soft. Beat in the eggs, then the grated potatoes, chives or parsley, and salt and pepper to taste.

Pour enough oil into a deep frying pan to come about 2.5 cm/1 inch up the sides of the pan.

Place the pan over moderate heat until the oil is sizzling hot, then drop the potato mixture into the hot oil 1 × 15 spoon/1 tablespoon at a time, spacing them well apart. Fry for about 5 minutes until golden brown on each side, turning them once, then remove from the oil with a slotted spoon. Drain on paper towels and keep hot while frying the remainder.

Serve instead of French fries with grills, fried fish or Tournedos de Dijon (page 41).
Makes 20–24

Tomates niçoises; Aubergines à l'ail; Pommes de terre soufflées; Beignets de pommes de terre

Beignets de chou-fleur
Cauliflower fritters

Metric	Imperial
1 × 1 kg cauliflower, stalks removed and divided into florets	1 × 2 lb cauliflower, stalks removed and divided into florets
salt	salt
1 × 15 ml spoon lemon juice	1 tablespoon lemon juice
vegetable oil, for deep-frying	vegetable oil, for deep-frying

Fritter batter:	Fritter batter:
115 g plain flower	4½ oz plain flour
1 × 1.25 ml spoon cayenne pepper	¼ teaspoon cayenne pepper
2 eggs, beaten	2 eggs, beaten
150 ml milk	¼ pint milk
1 × 15 ml spoon melted butter	1 tablespoon melted butter

Preparation time: 15 minutes, plus standing
Cooking time: about 20 minutes

For a starter serve these fritters with tartare sauce or a freshly made tomato sauce which has plenty of flavour – the tomato sauce recipe with Timbale au Jambon (page 29), which is made with onions and garlic, is ideal.

Plunge the cauliflower florets into a large pan of boiling salted water, swirl in the lemon juice, then bring the water back to the boil. Lower the heat and simmer for 2 minutes. Drain thoroughly and cool.
Meanwhile, make the fritter batter. Sift the flour, cayenne and a pinch of salt into a bowl and make a well in the centre. Pour in the eggs, then whisk vigorously with a wire balloon whisk, gradually whisking in half the milk and incorporating the flour from the sides into the centre. Pour in the remaining milk and whisk again until the batter is smooth. Stir in the melted butter.
Stir the cooled cauliflower into the batter, cover and leave to stand for 15–20 minutes, stirring frequently. Heat the oil in a deep-fat frier to 190°C/375°F or until a stale bread cube turns golden in 40–50 seconds. Remove a few of the cauliflower florets from the bowl of batter with a slotted spoon and deep-fry in the hot oil for 2–3 minutes until light golden in colour. Drain on paper towels and keep hot while quickly frying the remainder. Serve immediately, together with the crisp pieces of batter that collect in the pan during frying.
Serve with roasts or as a starter.
Serves 4–6

Epinards aux pignons
Spinach with pine nuts and raisins

Metric	Imperial
1 kg fresh spinach	2 lb fresh spinach
salt	salt
3 × 15 ml spoons olive oil	3 tablespoons olive oil
50 g pine nuts or flaked almonds	2 oz pine nuts or flaked almonds
100 g seedless raisins	4 oz seedless raisins
freshly ground black pepper	freshly ground black pepper

Preparation time: about 30 minues
Cooking time: about 25 minutes

If fresh spinach is not available, use 450 g/1 lb frozen whole leaf spinach; defrost and cook according to packet instructions, then add to the pan of nuts and raisins as with the fresh spinach.

Wash the spinach carefully under cold running water, discarding tough discoloured leaves and large coarse stalks. Put in a large pan with only the water clinging to the leaves. Sprinkle with 1 × 5 ml spoon/1 teaspoon salt and heat gently until the juices flow from the spinach. Cover the pan with a tight-fitting lid and cook gently for about 8 minutes, shaking the pan constantly.
Drain the spinach very thoroughly, then turn on to a board or work surface and chop roughly.
Heat the oil in a large frying pan, add the pine nuts, or almonds, and raisins and fry over moderate heat for about 5 minutes. Stir constantly until the nuts turn golden.
Add the spinach to the pan and stir to mix with the nuts and raisins. Add salt and pepper to taste and continue frying and stirring until the spinach is heated through. Transfer to a warmed serving dish.
Serve with all meats, especially Filet de Porc Tourangeau (page 44), Porc au Lait (page 45), and Tournedos de Dijon (page 41). This vegetable dish also goes well with omelettes.

Epinards aux pignons; Beignets de chou-fleur; Haricots verts au lard

Haricots verts au lard
French beans with bacon

Metric
450 g French beans,
   topped and tailed
salt
4 rashers streaky bacon,
   rinds removed, cut into
   thin strips
2 shallots or 1 small
   onion, peeled and finely
   chopped
2 eggs
1 × 15 ml spoon wine
   vinegar
freshly ground black
   pepper
freshly chopped savory or
   parsley, to garnish
   (optional)

Imperial
1 lb French beans, topped
   and tailed
salt
4 rashers streaky bacon,
   rinds removed, cut into
   thin strips
2 shallots or 1 small
   onion, peeled and finely
   chopped
2 eggs
1 tablespoon wine
   vinegar
freshly ground black
   pepper
freshly chopped savory or
   parsley, to garnish
   (optional)

Preparation time: about 15 minutes
Cooking time: about 30–35 minutes

Plunge the beans into a large pan of boiling salted water, bring quickly back to the boil, then lower the heat and simmer for about 15 minutes or until the beans are tender.

Meanwhile, put the bacon pieces in a heavy-based pan and fry over gentle heat until the fat runs from the bacon. Add the shallots or onion and continue frying until both bacon and shallots are lightly coloured. Put the eggs and vinegar in a bowl with 1 × 15 ml spoon/1 tablespoon boiling water from the beans. Beat well to mix.

Drain the beans, then stir them into the bacon and onions. Pour in the egg mixture and stir over moderate heat until the mixture is creamy and coats the beans. Add salt and pepper to taste, then transfer to a warmed serving dish.

Serve with egg and cheese dishes, chicken or meat, and especially Paupiettes de Boeuf (page 42) and Filet de Porc Tourangeau (page 44).

Croquettes de panais
Parsnip croquettes

Preparation time: about 45 minutes, plus chilling
Cooking time: about 35 minutes

Metric	**Imperial**
450 g parsnips, peeled and cut into chunks	1 lb parsnips, peeled and cut into chunks
2 medium potatoes, peeled and halved	2 medium potatoes, peeled and halved
salt	salt
50 g plain flour	2 oz plain flour
25 g butter, softened	1 oz butter, softened
freshly ground black pepper	freshly ground black pepper
vegetable oil, for deep frying	vegetable oil, for deep frying

Coating:	**Coating:**
about 2 × 15 ml spoons plain flour	about 2 tablespoons plain flour
1 large egg, beaten	1 large egg, beaten
75 g dried breadcrumbs	3 oz dried breadcrumbs
25 g blanched almonds, finely chopped	1 oz blanched almonds, finely chopped

Cook the parsnips and potatoes in a pan of boiling salted water for about 20 minutes until tender. Drain thoroughly, then return to the rinsed-out pan and place over gentle heat to remove excess moisture. Stir constantly to prevent the vegetables catching on the bottom of the pan.

Transfer the vegetables to a bowl and leave to cool slightly, then mash until smooth. Beat in the flour, butter, and salt and pepper to taste until evenly mixed. With well-floured hands, form the mixture into 8 croquette shapes. Coat with the flour, dip first into the beaten egg, then into the breadcrumbs mixed with the chopped almonds. When evenly and thoroughly coated, chill the croquettes in the refrigerator for at least 1 hour.

Heat the oil in a deep-fat fryer to 190°C/375°F or until a stale bread cube turns golden in 40–50 seconds. Lower a few of the croquettes carefully into the hot oil, then deep-fry for about 5 minutes until they are golden brown on all sides. Drain on paper towels and keep hot while frying the remainder.

Serve immediately with roasts and grills, particularly beef and steaks.

Topinambours aux tomates
Jerusalem artichokes with tomatoes

Preparation time: 30 minutes
Cooking time: about 50 minutes

Metric	**Imperial**
1 kg Jerusalem artichokes	2 lb Jerusalem artichokes
salt	salt
juice of 1 lemon	juice of 1 lemon
25 g butter	1 oz butter
2 × 15 ml spoons olive oil	2 tablespoons olive oil
1 medium onion, peeled and thinly sliced	1 medium onion, peeled and thinly sliced
1–2 garlic cloves, peeled and crushed with 1 × 2.5 ml spoon salt	1–2 garlic cloves, peeled and crushed with ½ teaspoon salt
225 g tomatoes, skinned, seeded and chopped	8 oz tomatoes, skinned seeded and chopped
2 × 5 ml spoons freshly chopped basil or 1 × 5 ml spoon dried basil	2 teaspoons freshly chopped basil or 1 teaspoon dried basil
freshly ground black pepper	freshly ground black pepper

Put the artichokes in a large pan of salted water to which the lemon juice has been added. Bring to the boil, then lower the heat, cover and simmer for 7 minutes. Drain and leave until cool enough to handle. Meanwhile, melt the butter with the oil in a separate pan, add the onion and garlic and fry gently until soft and lightly coloured. Stir in the tomatoes, basil, and salt and pepper to taste, then simmer over very gentle heat for about 5 minutes, stirring occasionally to break up the tomatoes.

Peel the artichokes and slice thickly. Stir into the tomato mixture until coated, then cover and simmer very gently for about 30 minutes or until the artichokes are tender. Stir occasionally during this time to prevent the artichokes from catching on the bottom of the pan, and if necessary stir in a little water from time to time. Taste and adjust the seasoning. Put into a warmed serving dish and serve immediately.

Serve with roast lamb, pork and beef.

Clockwise from top left: Croquettes de panais; Carottes vichyssoises; Topinambours aux tomates

Carottes vichyssoises
Carrots with Vichy water

Metric
25 g butter
1 onion, peeled and
    finely chopped
450 g carrots, peeled
    and cut into matchstick
    strips
300 ml Vichy water
1 × 5 ml spoon sugar
salt
4 × 15 ml spoons
    double cream
2 × 15 ml spoons freshly
    chopped parsely
freshly ground black
    pepper

Imperial
1 oz butter
1 onion, peeled and
    finely chopped
1 lb carrots, peeled
    and cut into matchstick
    strips
½ pint Vichy water
1 teaspoon sugar
salt
4 tablespoons double
    cream
2 tablespoons freshly
    chopped parsley
freshly ground black
    pepper

Preparation time: about 20 minutes
Cooking time: about 40 minutes

This is a classic recipe in which carrots are cooked in natural spring water from Vichy in France. It is an ideal way to use up Vichy water from bottles which have been opened.
Alternatively use half the amount of Vichy water and make up the full quantity of liquid with chicken stock.

Melt the butter in a large heavy-based pan. Add the onion and fry gently until soft and lightly coloured, then add the carrots and stir until coated in the butter and onion. Pour in the Vichy water.
Bring to the boil, then lower the heat and add the sugar and 1 × 2.5 ml spoon/½ teaspoon salt. Simmer continuously for about 30 minutes or until the carrots are tender and all the liquid has been absorbed.
Stir in the cream and parsley, then add salt to taste and plenty of pepper. Transfer to a warmed serving dish. Serve immediately with roast meat, particularly lamb or with chops.

Courgettes au citron vert
Courgettes with lime

Metric
25 g butter
2 × 15 ml spoons olive
  oil
1 medium onion, peeled
  and thinly sliced
1–2 garlic cloves,
  peeled and crushed
  with 1 × 2.5 ml spoon
  salt
450 g courgettes, sliced
juice of 1 lime
salt
freshly ground black
  pepper

Imperial
1 oz butter
2 tablespoons olive
  oil
1 medium onion, peeled
  and thinly sliced
1–2 garlic cloves,
  peeled and crushed
  with ½ teaspoon
  salt
1 lb courgettes, sliced
juice of 1 lime
salt
freshly ground black
  pepper

Preparation time: 10–15 minutes
Cooking time: 15 minutes

If fresh limes are difficult to obtain, bottled lime juice for cooking is available at some large supermarkets and good delicatessens. You will need about 2 × 15 ml spoons/2 tablespoons. Do not be tempted to cook the courgettes for longer than the exact time stated – they should have a 'bite' to them.

Melt the butter with the oil in a large frying pan. Add the onion and garlic and fry gently until soft and lightly coloured.
Add the courgettes, increase the heat and fry briskly for 10 minutes only, turning them over and shaking the pan constantly. Stir in the lime juice, add salt to taste and plenty of pepper, then turn into a warmed serving dish.
Serve with rich meat dishes, especially pork and veal in creamy sauces, or with oily fish.

Gratin de chou
Cabbage and bacon pie

Metric
1 medium white cabbage
  (about 1 kg)
salt
3 × 15 ml spoons olive oil
225 g back bacon, rind
  removed, chopped
1 medium onion, peeled
  and finely chopped
1–2 garlic cloves, peeled
  and crushed with 1 ×
  2.5 ml spoon salt
2 eggs
150 ml milk
50 g fresh white
  breadcrumbs
100 g Gruyère cheese,
  grated
freshly ground black
  pepper

Imperial
1 medium white cabbage
  (about 2 lb)
salt
3 tablespoons olive oil
8 oz back bacon, rind
  removed, chopped
1 medium onion, peeled
  and finely chopped
1–2 garlic cloves, peeled
  and crushed with ½
  teaspoon salt
2 eggs
¼ pint milk
2 oz fresh white
  breadcrumbs
4 oz Gruyère cheese,
  grated
freshly ground black
  pepper

Preparation time: 40 minutes
Cooking time: about 1¼ hours
Oven: 190°C, 375°F, Gas Mark 5

Remove 8 large unbroken leaves from the outside of the cabbage. Plunge into a pan of boiling salted water, bring back to the boil and boil for 5 minutes. Drain thoroughly.
Heat 1 × 15 ml spoon/1 tablespoon oil in a large frying pan, add the bacon and fry over moderate heat until the fat begins to run from the bacon. Add the onion and garlic and continue frying over moderate heat until the bacon and onion are both lightly coloured, stirring constantly. Remove from the pan with a slotted spoon and set aside on paper towels.
Chop half the inner leaves from the cabbage. Heat the remaining oil in the pan, add the chopped leaves and fry for a further 5 minutes, stirring frequently.
Meanwhile, put the eggs in a bowl and beat together lightly with the milk, breadcrumbs, cheese, and salt and pepper to taste. Remove the cabbage mixture from the pan with a slotted spoon and stir into the egg mixture with the bacon and onion.
Place 6 drained outer cabbage leaves in the bottom of a well-buttered shallow 1.2 litre/2 pint baking dish. Overlap them slightly so that they line the dish. Spoon the stuffing mixture into the dish, then fold the leaves over the stuffing. Cover with the remaining 2 cabbage leaves to enclose the stuffing completely.
Bake, uncovered, in a preheated oven for 45 minutes or until the cabbage mixture is set in the centre when pierced with a knife. Remove from the oven and leave to stand for 5 minutes, then unmould on to a warmed serving platter.
Serve hot with sausages or a mixed grill as a lunch or supper dish.

Courgettes dauphinoises
Courgettes with cheese and cream

Preparation time: about 15 minutes
Cooking time: 40–45 minutes
Oven: 200°C, 400°F, Gas Mark 6

Metric
50 g butter
1 medium onion, peeled
    and thinly sliced
450 g courgettes, sliced
2 eggs
300 ml double cream
1 × 1.25 ml spoon freshly
    grated nutmeg
salt
freshly ground black
    pepper
50 g Gruyère cheese,
    grated

Imperial
2 oz butter
1 medium onion, peeled
    and thinly sliced
1 lb courgettes, sliced
2 eggs
½ pint double cream
¼ teaspoon freshly grated
    nutmeg
salt
freshly ground black
    pepper
2 oz Gruyère cheese,
    grated

Melt half the butter in a large frying pan, add the sliced onion and fry gently until soft. Remove with a slotted spoon and place in a buttered ovenproof dish. Melt the remaining butter in the pan, add the courgette slices and fry for about 10 minutes until golden brown on both sides, turning them frequently. Transfer to the dish and mix with the onions.
In a bowl, beat the eggs well to mix, then beat in the cream, nutmeg, and salt and pepper to taste. Pour over the courgettes and onions, then sprinkle the Gruyère cheese evenly over the top. Bake uncovered in a preheated oven for 20–25 minutes or until the custard is set and the topping is golden and bubbling. Serve hot with any meat, or simply with French bread for a lunch dish.

Clockwise from top: Courgettes dauphinoises; Courgettes au citron vert; Gratin de chou

DESSERTS AND PÂTISSERIE

Glancing in the window of any pâtisserie in France, it seems hard to believe that the French prefer to end most everyday meals with cheese and fresh fruit! The spectacular looking tarts with their rows of fresh soft fruits glistening with sweet, shiny glaze, and the gorgeous gâteaux and pâtisserie simply oozing with cream, these are reserved for special occasions only. Not that the French cook never makes his or her own desserts and gâteaux, it is simply an admission that these things are, in the main, best left to the experts. Custards and compôtes are made at home, however, so too are crêpes and mousses, but generally only at weekends and on holidays. For the rest of the year the family is more than content with fresh fruit and cheese.

Sorbet au cassis
Blackcurrant sorbet

Metric
100 g sugar
300 ml plus 2 × 15 ml
  spoons water
1 × 2.5 ml spoon
  powdered gelatine
225 g fresh or frozen
  blackcurrants, topped
  and tailed
2 × 5 ml spoons lemon
  juice
1 egg white
wafers or dessert biscuits,
  to serve (optional)

Imperial
4 oz sugar
½ pint plus 2 tablespoons
  water
½ teaspoon powdered
  gelatine
8 oz fresh or frozen
  blackcurrants, topped
  and tailed
2 teaspoons lemon
  juice
1 egg white
wafers or dessert biscuits,
  to serve (optional)

Preparation time: 30 minutes, plus freezing
Cooking time: 25–30 minutes

This sorbet can be made in a home freezer, or in the freezing compartment of the refrigerator, turned to the coldest setting about 1 hour before starting the recipe. When breaking up the half-frozen mixture, use a fork, not an electric or rotary beater, as these overbeat the mixture which will increase the volume too much and give a diluted or runny result.

Put the sugar and 300 ml/½ pint water in a heavy-based pan and heat gently until the sugar has dissolved, stirring occasionally. Bring to the boil and boil for 10 minutes until syrupy, then remove from the heat and leave to cool.
Sprinkle the gelatine over the remaining 2 × 15 ml spoons/2 tablespoons water in a heatproof bowl. Leave until spongy, then place the bowl in a pan of gently simmering water. Heat gently until the gelatine has dissolved, stirring occasionally, then remove from the heat and stir into the sugar syrup.
Put the blackcurrants in a pan with the lemon juice and heat gently for 5–10 minutes until softened. Cool slightly, purée in an electric blender, then push through a sieve to remove all seeds and skins.
Combine the sugar syrup and blackcurrant purée in a bowl until well mixed, then transfer to a freezer-proof container. Freeze, uncovered, for about 3 hours until firm round the edges.
Remove the mixture from the freezer and break up with a fork. Whisk the egg white until stiff and standing in peaks, then fold into the blackcurrant mixture until evenly incorporated. Return to the freezer container, cover and freeze overnight.
To serve, remove from the freezer and leave to stand at room temperature for about 30 minutes until soft enough to scoop. Serve in individual glasses, with wafers or dessert biscuits such as langues de chats.

Sorbet au cassis; Tonille aux framboises

Tonille aux framboises
Almond shortcake with raspberries

Metric
75 g flaked almonds,
  toasted
100 g unsalted butter
75 g caster sugar
150 g plain flour

Filling:
450 ml double cream
50 g icing sugar, sifted
finely grated rind of 1
  orange
2 × 5 ml spoons orange
  juice
350 g fresh or frozen
  raspberries, hulled

Imperial
3 oz flaked almonds,
  toasted
4 oz unsalted butter
3 oz caster sugar
5 oz plain flour

Filling:
¾ pint double cream
2 oz icing sugar, sifted
finely grated rind of 1
  orange
2 teaspoons orange
  juice
12 oz fresh or frozen
  raspberries, hulled

Preparation time: about 1 hour, plus chilling
Cooking time: 15–20 minutes
Oven: 190°C, 375°F, Gas Mark 5

Ground toasted hazelnuts can replace the almonds and strawberries or peaches can be used instead of raspberries.

To make the shortcake, grind the almonds in an electric grinder or food processor. Set aside.
Put the butter and sugar in a bowl and beat together until light and fluffy. Beat in the flour, then the almonds to make a smooth dough, then form into 3 equal balls. Wrap in foil or cling film and chill in the refrigerator for at least 30 minutes until firm.
With floured fingers, press each ball of dough flat into a 20 cm/8 inch round on a baking sheet lined with non-stick silicone paper, using 2 or 3 baking sheets if necessary.
Bake in a preheated oven, in batches if necessary, for 15–20 minutes until the shortcake is light golden in colour. Remove from the oven and cut 1 round into 6 equal triangles, spacing them slightly apart. Leave to cool on the baking sheets for 10 minutes, then carefully transfer to a wire tray to cool completely.
To make the filling, whip the cream until stiff with 40 g/1½ oz icing sugar, the orange rind and juice. Crush the raspberries lightly, reserving a few whole ones for decoration, then fold lightly into the cream.
To serve, place 1 shortcake round on a serving plate and spread with half the raspberry cream. Place another shortcake on top and spread with the remaining cream. Arrange the triangles of shortcake on top, tilting them upward in the centre so that they fit neatly and a little of the raspberry cream is visible between each triangle. Decorate with the reserved raspberries and dust with the reserved icing sugar.
Serves 6

Clafoutis
Cherry batter pudding

Preparation time: 20 minutes, plus soaking
Cooking time: 25–30 minutes
Oven: 200°C, 400°F, Gas Mark 6

Metric
450 g black cherries,
    pitted
4 × 15 ml spoons brandy
    or Kirsch
75 g plain flour
pinch of salt
75 g caster sugar
2 eggs
2 egg yolks
about 450 ml milk
2 × 15 ml spoons melted
    butter
icing sugar, to serve

Imperial
1 lb black cherries,
    pitted
4 tablespoons brandy
    or Kirsch
3 oz plain flour
pinch of salt
3 oz caster sugar
2 eggs
2 egg yolks
about ¾ pint milk
2 tablespoons melted
    butter
icing sugar, to serve

If fresh black cherries are not available, use 2 × 425 g/15 oz cans of cherries, well drained, and if they are sweetened, decrease the amount of sugar to 25 g/1 oz. Use a cherry pitter to remove the stones because the fruit will not hold its shape during cooking if it is halved.

Put the cherries in a bowl and sprinkle over half the brandy or Kirsch. Leave to soak for 1 hour.
Sift the flour and salt into a bowl and stir in the sugar. Make a well in the centre, add the whole eggs, egg yolks and 300 ml/½ pint milk, and beat, gradually drawing in the flour from the sides of the bowl, until smooth.
Drain the cherries and make up the juice to 150 ml/¼ pint with milk. Whisk this mixture into the batter until smooth, then whisk in the melted butter.
Place the cherries in a shallow baking dish. Pour on the batter, then bake in a preheated oven for 25–30 minutes until puffed up and light golden.
Remove from the oven, sprinkle with the remaining brandy or Kirsch, then leave in a warm place for about 15–20 minutes, by which time the clafoutis will have shrunk slightly. Serve warm, dusted lightly with the icing sugar.

Tarte au citron
Lemon tart

Metric	Imperial
125 g plain flour	*5 oz plain flour*
pinch of salt	*pinch of salt*
2 × 15 ml spoons caster sugar	*2 tablespoons caster sugar*
100 g butter, chilled	*4 oz butter, chilled*
1 egg yolk	*1 egg yolk*
1 × 5 ml spoon lemon juice	*1 teaspoon lemon juice*
1–2 × 5 ml spoons icing sugar, to finish	*1–2 teaspoons icing sugar, to finish*

Filling:

Metric	Imperial
75 g unsalted butter	*3 oz unsalted butter*
75 g caster sugar	*3 oz caster sugar*
100 g ground almonds	*4 oz ground almonds*
2 egg yolks	*2 egg yolks*
finely grated rind and juice of 1 large lemon	*finely grated rind and juice of 1 large lemon*
3 egg whites	*3 egg whites*

Preparation time: 45 minutes, plus chilling
Cooking time: 35–40 minutes
Oven: 190°C, 375°F, Gas Mark 5;
       160°C, 325°F, Gas Mark 3

With its sharp, tangy flavour, this lemon tart is excellent served warm as a dessert or cold as pâtisserie with coffee. The pastry base, known as pâte sablée in French, is extra rich and sweet, more of a biscuit crust than a pastry. Because of its richness it is difficult to roll out; and it is sometimes easier, therefore, to press it into the flan tin or ring with the fingertips.

Sift the flour and salt into a bowl and stir in the sugar. Cut the butter into the flour in small pieces, then rub in lightly with the fingertips. Mix the egg yolk and lemon juice together, then stir into the flour mixture with a round-bladed knife until the mixture draws together. Form into a smooth ball with one hand, then cover and chill in the refrigerator for 30 minutes.
Roll out the dough on a floured surface and use to line a loose-bottomed fluted 20 cm/8 inch flan tin or flan ring set on a baking sheet. Prick the base of the dough in several places with a fork, then line with foil or greaseproof paper and fill with baking beans.
Bake the pastry case 'blind' in a preheated oven for 10 minutes, then remove the paper and beans. Lightly beat a little egg white from the filling and brush over the base of the dough. Return to the oven and bake for a further 10 minutes, then remove and set aside. Reduce the oven temperature.
To make the filling, put the butter and sugar in a bowl and beat together until light and fluffy. Beat in the almonds, egg yolks and lemon rind and juice until evenly mixed. In a separate bowl, whisk the egg whites until stiff and standing in peaks. Fold the egg whites gently into the lemon mixture then spoon into the pastry case.
Bake in the oven for 15–20 minutes until a skewer inserted in the centre comes out clean. Remove from the oven and sift icing sugar evenly over the top. Leave to cool slightly, then remove the flan tin or ring and place on a serving plate. Serve warm or cold.
Serves 4–6

Clafoutis; Tarte au citron

Gâteau pithiviers
Puff pastry gâteau

Metric	Imperial
100 g unsalted butter, softened	4 oz unsalted butter, softened
100 g caster sugar	4 oz caster sugar
1 egg, beaten with 1 egg yolk	1 egg, beaten with 1 egg yolk
100 g ground almonds	4 oz ground almonds
2 × 15 ml spoons rum	2 tablespoons rum
1 × 400 g packet frozen puff pastry, defrosted	1 × 14 oz packet frozen puff pastry, defrosted

Glaze:	Glaze:
1 egg, beaten	1 egg, beaten
a little icing sugar	a little icing sugar

Preparation time: 45 minutes
Cooking time: 30–35 minutes
Oven: 220°C, 425°F, Gas Mark 7

Put the butter and sugar in a bowl and beat together until light and fluffy. Beat in the egg and egg yolk mixture, then beat in the almonds and rum until evenly mixed. Set aside.

Roll out half the pastry on a floured surface to a 23 cm/9 inch circle. Place the circle on a dampened baking sheet. Spread the filling over the circle to within about 1 cm/½ inch of the edge, mounding it up in the centre. Brush the exposed edge of the pastry with water.

Roll out the remaining pastry to a 25 cm/10 inch circle. Cut away a narrow strip all round the edge of this circle. Press this strip around the moistened edge of the circle on the baking sheet. Brush the strip with water. Cover the filling with the second circle of pastry, pressing it down firmly at the edge to seal. Knock up the edge with the back of a knife, then give the edge a scalloped effect by pressing your thumb around it at regular intervals and marking in between each thumb mark with the back of the knife. Make a hole in the centre of the gâteau with a skewer, and brush all over the pastry with the beaten egg, taking care not to brush the decorated edge or the pastry will not rise. With a sharp knife, make shallow semi-circular cuts in the pastry all round the top of the gâteau, working from the centre towards the outside edge.

Bake in a preheated oven for 25–30 minutes until puffed up and golden brown, then sift the icing sugar evenly over the top of the gâteau and return to the oven for a further 5 minutes until glazed and shiny. Leave to stand on the baking sheet for a few minutes, then carefully transfer to a wire rack. Serve warm or cold with cream.
Serves 4–6

Tarte tatin
Upside-down apple pie

Metric	Imperial
125 g plain flour	5 oz plain flour
pinch of salt	pinch of salt
2 × 15 ml spoons caster sugar	2 tablespoons caster sugar
100 g butter, chilled	4 oz butter, chilled
1 egg yolk	1 egg yolk
3 × 5 ml spoons lemon juice	3 teaspoons lemon juice
1 kg cooking apples	2 lb cooking apples
100 g unsalted butter	4 oz unsalted butter
100 g sugar	4 oz sugar

Preparation time: about 45 minutes, plus chilling
Cooking time: 55 minutes
Oven: 190°C, 375°F, Gas Mark 5

Sift the flour and salt into a bowl and stir in the sugar. Cut the butter into small pieces, then rub lightly into the flour. Mix the egg yolk and 1 × 5 ml spoon/1 teaspoon lemon juice together, then stir into the flour mixture with a round-bladed knife until the mixture draws together. Form into a smooth ball with one hand, then chill in the refrigerator for 30 minutes.

Meanwhile, peel and core the apples and slice thinly. Place them in a bowl of ice-cold water and stir in the remaining lemon juice. Melt the butter gently in a 1 litre/2 pint flameproof pie dish. Pour off all but about 2 × 15 ml spoons/2 tablespoons melted butter and reserve. Brush the butter remaining in the dish around the base and sides of it. Sprinkle the base with about one-quarter of the sugar, then continue heating gently until the butter and sugar mixture sizzles and turns a golden-brown, caramel colour.

Drain the apple slices thoroughly. Arrange a single layer of apple slices in the dish, overlapping them in circles. Drizzle over a little of the reserved melted butter and sprinkle with sugar. Continue these layers, finishing with a layer of sugar.

Roll out the dough on a floured surface and use to cover the top of the pie dish, tucking the edges inside the rim of the dish to enclose the apples completely. Make a small hole in the centre of the pastry, then bake in a preheated oven for about 45 minutes until the apples are tender. If the pastry becomes over-brown during baking, cover it with foil.

To serve, leave the pie to stand in a warm place for 5–10 minutes. Loosen the edges by carefully running a knife between the pie and the dish. Invert on to a warmed serving plate and serve immediately, with pouring cream.

Compôte de trois fruits
Three-fruit compôte

Metric	Imperial
100 g sugar	*4 oz sugar*
300 ml dry white wine	*½ pint dry white wine*
150 ml water	*¼ pint water*
1 vanilla pod	*1 vanilla pod*
4 ripe cooking pears	*4 ripe cooking pears*
1 medium pineapple (about 1 kg)	*1 medium pineapple (about 2 lb)*
175 g black grapes, pips removed	*6 oz black grapes, pips removed*
2 × 15 ml spoons brandy (optional)	*2 tablespoons brandy (optional)*

Preparation time: 30 minutes, plus chilling
Cooking time: 40–45 minutes

Put the sugar, wine, water and vanilla pod in a large heavy-based pan. Heat gently until the sugar has dissolved, stirring occasionally, then bring to the boil. Boil vigorously for 5 minutes, then lower the heat and simmer gently.

Peel, core and quarter the pears. Poach them gently in the syrup in the covered pan for 10–15 minutes, spooning the liquid over them occasionally.

Meanwhile, slice the pineapple into rings, discarding the crown. Peel and core the pineapple rings. Add the pineapple to the pan with the grapes, cover again and poach gently for a further 10 minutes until all the fruits are tender. Leave to cool, covered.

Remove the vanilla pod, then sprinkle in the brandy (if using). Carefully transfer the fruit to a serving bowl. Serve warm or cover with cling film and chill in the refrigerator for at least 4 hours before serving.

Gâteau pithiviers; Compôte de trois fruits; Tarte tatin

Charlotte au chocolat
Chocolate charlotte

Metric	Imperial
225 g plain dessert chocolate, broken into pieces	8 oz plain dessert chocolate, broken into pieces
about 6 × 15 ml spoons rum	about 6 tablespoons rum
100 g unsalted butter, softened	4 oz unsalted butter, softened
225 g ground almonds	8 oz ground almonds
oil for preparing mould	oil for preparing mould
about 20 sponge fingers	about 20 sponge fingers
300 ml double cream	½ pint double cream

Decoration:

Metric	Imperial
120 ml double or whipping cream	4 fl oz double or whipping cream
25 g plain dessert chocolate, grated	1 oz plain dessert chocolate, grated

Preparation time: about 1 hour, plus chilling
Cooking time: about 5 minutes

Use the best quality dessert chocolate available; good delicatessens and some large supermarkets sell blocks of French dessert chocolate, which are ideal.
For a prettier effect, and to help keep the sponge fingers in place before serving, tie a ribbon around the middle of the charlotte, finishing with a bow.

Put the chocolate and 2 × 15 ml spoons/2 tablespoons rum in a heatproof bowl standing over a pan of gently simmering water. Heat gently until the chocolate has melted, stirring once or twice. Remove from the heat and work in the butter gradually until melted, then stir in the almonds. Leave to cool.
Meanwhile, line the base of a 900 ml/1½ pint charlotte mould with non-stick silicone or greaseproof paper. Brush the paper and inside the rim of the mould lightly with oil. Dip the sponge fingers one at a time into the remaining rum, then use to line the sides of the mould, standing them sugared side outward and as close together as possible. Trim them to fit if necessary.
Whip the cream until just firm, then fold into the chocolate mixture. Spoon into the mould and level the surface, then cover and chill in the refrigerator overnight.
The next day, turn the charlotte out of the mould on to a serving plate. Whip the cream for decoration and pipe or swirl decoratively on top and round the charlotte. Sprinkle the grated chocolate over the top, then chill in the refrigerator until serving time. Serve chilled with single cream.
Serves 8

Chocolat bavarois à l'orange
Chocolate cream with orange

Metric	Imperial
600 ml milk	1 pint milk
100 g plain dessert chocolate, finely grated	4 oz plain dessert chocolate, finely grated
4 egg yolks	4 egg yolks
75 g caster sugar	3 oz caster sugar
grated zest of 2 oranges	grated zest of 2 oranges
1 envelope (15 g) powdered gelatine	1 envelope (½ oz) powdered gelatine
juice of 1 large orange	juice of 1 large orange
2 × 15 ml spoons orange-flavoured liqueur	2 tablespoons orange-flavoured liqueur
150 ml double cream	¼ pint double cream

Preparation time: 30 minutes, plus cooling and chilling
Cooking time: about 30 minutes

For the flavour of this sumptuous dessert cooking chocolate or chocolate cake covering are not suitable; buy the best quality dessert chocolate available. If preferred, you can fold in 2 stiffly beaten egg whites after the cream for a lighter, less rich result.

Put the milk and chocolate in a heavy-based pan and heat gently, stirring, until the chocolate has melted. Meanwhile, put the egg yolks, sugar and orange zest in a large bowl and beat until the sugar has dissolved. Gradually pour the hot milk and melted chocolate into the egg yolk mixture, stirring constantly. Return this mixture to the pan and heat very gently until the custard thickens and coats the back of a wooden spoon. Stir constantly and do not let the custard boil or it will separate. Remove from the heat and set aside. Sprinkle the gelatine over the orange juice in a heatproof bowl. Leave until spongy, then place the bowl in a pan of gently simmering water. Heat gently until the gelatine has dissolved, stirring occasionally. Remove from the heat and leave to cool slightly, then stir gradually into the chocolate custard with the liqueur. Leave until the custard is completely cold and just beginning to thicken, whisking occasionally to prevent a skin forming on the top.
Whip the cream until just firm, then fold into the cold custard. Pour into a wetted 1.2 litres/2 pint mould, cover and chill in the refrigerator overnight.
To serve, loosen the custard by pulling the top edge away from the mould with your fingertips, then invert the custard on to a serving plate. (If it is difficult to unmould, dip the base of the mould into a bowl of hot water for a few seconds.) Serve chilled.
Serves 6

Top: Chocolat bavarois à l'orange; Charlotte au chocolat

Pêches à la bordelaise
Peaches marinated in red wine

Metric	Imperial
300 ml red Bordeaux wine	½ pint red Bordeaux wine
100 g sugar	4 oz sugar
1 cinnamon stick	1 cinnamon stick
4 ripe peaches	4 ripe peaches
25–50 g flaked almonds, toasted	1–2 oz flaked almonds, toasted
dessert biscuits, to serve	dessert biscuits, to serve

Preparation time: 20 minutes, plus chilling

Put the wine in a pan, add the sugar and heat gently until the sugar has dissolved, stirring occasionally. Add the cinnamon stick and bring to the boil. Remove from the heat and cool.

Plunge the peaches into a bowl of boiling water, leave for 10 seconds, then remove with a slotted spoon and peel off the skins. Halve the fruit, remove the stones and slice the flesh thickly. Place the slices in a bowl, then strain in the wine. Cover the surface of the liquid closely with a saucer or small plate (to prevent the peaches floating in the liquid), then chill in the refrigerator for at least 4 hours.

Divide the peaches and wine amongst 4 glasses and sprinkle with the almonds. Serve chilled, with dessert biscuits such as langues de chats.

Fraises cardinales
Strawberries with raspberry sauce

Metric	Imperial
450 g fresh raspberries or 350 g frozen raspberries, defrosted	1 lb fresh raspberries or 12 oz frozen raspberries, defrosted
finely grated rind and juice of 1 orange	finely grated rind and juice of 1 orange
4 × 15 ml spoons orange-flavoured liqueur (optional)	4 tablespoons orange-flavoured liqueur (optional)
450–700 g fresh strawberries, hulled	1–1½ lb fresh strawberries, hulled
50–75 g caster sugar	2–3 oz caster sugar
4 orange slices, to decorate	4 orange slices, to decorate

Preparation time: about 20 minutes, plus chilling

Work the raspberries through a fine sieve, or purée in an electric blender, then sieve to remove the seeds. Stir the orange rind and juice into the purée, with the liqueur (if using).

Halve the strawberries or slice them if large. Place a few strawberries in the bottom of 4 individual glasses or bowls and sprinkle with sugar to taste. Pour over a little of the raspberry sauce. Repeat these three layers until all the ingredients are used. Decorate the top of each glass with a twist of orange, then chill in the refrigerator for at least 2 hours. Serve chilled.

Gâteau de crêpes aux abricots
Apricot pancake gâteau

Metric
100 g plain flour
pinch of salt
1 egg
300 ml milk
about 2 × 15 ml spoons
vegetable oil, for
frying

Imperial
4 oz plain flour
pinch of salt
1 egg
½ pint milk
about 2 tablespoons
vegetable oil, for
frying

Filling:
50–75 g sugar, or to
taste
150 ml water
4 × 15 ml spoons brandy
1 kg fresh apricots,
halved and stoned
50 g ratafias
pouring cream, to serve

Filling:
2–3 oz sugar, or to
taste
¼ pint water
4 tablespoons brandy
2 lb fresh apricots,
halved and stoned
2 oz ratafia
pouring cream, to serve

Gâteau de crêpes aux abricots; Pêches à la bordelaise;
Fraises cardinales

Preparation time: about 35 minutes, plus resting
Cooking time: 35–45 minutes

You can use the pancake batter in this recipe to make the classic Crêpes Suzette, as shown on the cover of this book. Add 1 × 5 ml spoon/1 teaspoon each tangerine or orange juice and Curaçao to the batter before frying. When the pancakes are made, spread each one with tangerine or orange butter made by creaming together equal quanties of butter and sugar with tangerine or orange juices, zest and Curaçao to taste. Fold the pancakes over the filling and place in a serving dish. Warm a little Curaçao, then pour over the pancakes and set alight. An alternative method of serving crêpes is to make a syrup from 100 g/4 oz each butter and sugar, with tangerine or orange juice, zest and Curaçao to taste. Fold the pancakes plain after frying, heat them in this syrup, then pour over warmed Curaçao and set alight.

Sift the flour and salt into a bowl. Make a well in the centre, add the egg, then gradually whisk in the milk until the batter is smooth. Cover and leave to stand for 30 minutes.
Meanwhile, make the filling. Put 50 g/2 oz sugar in a heavy-based pan with the water. Heat gently until the sugar has dissolved, then stir in half the brandy. Add the apricots and simmer gently for 10–15 minutes or until they are just tender. Remove with a slotted spoon, reserving the apricot syrup. Leave the apricots to cool slightly, then purée in an electric blender, reserving 6 whole ones for decoration.
Crush the ratafias finely, reserving a few whole ones. Make the pancakes. Heat a few drops of oil in a 15 cm/6 inch crêpe or frying pan until very hot. Pour in about one-eighth of the batter, tilting the pan so that the batter covers the base evenly. Cook for 1–2 minutes until set, then turn the crêpe over and cook for 1 minute on the other side. Slide the crêpe out of the pan on to a warm plate and cover with a sheet of greaseproof paper. Keep warm while making the remaining 7 crêpes, adding more oil when necessary. To assemble the gâteau, heat the apricot purée and the reserved apricot syrup gently in separate pans. Taste the purée for sweetness and add more sugar if necessary. Place one crêpe on a warmed serving platter and spread with about 1 × 15 ml spoon/1 tablespoon hot apricot purée. Sprinkle a little of the crushed ratafias over the top. Repeat these layers until all the pancakes, purée and crushed ratafias are used, finishing with a pancake.
Decorate the top of the gâteau with the reserved whole apricots and ratafias. Stir the remaining brandy into the hot apricot syrup. Serve the gâteau immediately, cut into wedges, with the sauce and cream handed in separate jugs.

Savarin aux fruits
Yeast ring cake with fruit

Metric
15 g fresh yeast
3 × 15 ml spoons
   lukewarm milk
100 g strong white flour
pinch of salt
1 × 5 ml spoon sugar
2 eggs, beaten
50 g butter, softened

Sugar syrup:
225 g sugar
300 ml water
4 × 15 ml spoons Kirsch,
   or to taste

Fruit filling:
2 bananas
100 g fresh strawberries,
   hulled and sliced
100 g fresh raspberries,
   hulled

Imperial
½ oz fresh yeast
3 tablespoons
   lukewarm milk
4 oz strong white flour
pinch of salt
1 teaspoon sugar
2 eggs, beaten
2 oz butter, softened

Sugar syrup:
8 oz sugar
½ pint water
4 tablespoons Kirsch,
   or to taste

Fruit filling:
2 bananas
4 oz fresh strawberries,
   hulled and sliced
4 oz fresh raspberries,
   hulled

Savarin aux fruits; Tarte aux pruneaux

Preparation time: about ¾ hour, plus rising
Cooking time: 25–30 minutes
Oven: 200°C, 400°F, Gas Mark 6

The savarin ring can be soaked in the sugar syrup overnight, and then filled with the fruit just before serving.

Cream the yeast in a bowl with the lukewarm milk, then gradually work in 25 g/1 oz flour. Leave to stand in a warm place for about 20 minutes until frothy, then add the remaining flour, salt, sugar, eggs and butter. Beat with a wooden spoon or whisk until an elasticated dough forms.

Put the mixture into a buttered and floured 20 cm/8 inch savarin or ring mould, then leave in a warm place for about 45 minutes until the mixture has risen almost to the top of the tin. Bake in a preheated oven for 25–30 minutes or until the savarin is golden on top and has shrunk away slightly from the sides of the tin. Meanwhile, make the sugar syrup. Put the sugar and water in a heavy-based pan and heat gently until the sugar has dissolved, stirring occasionally. Bring to the boil, simmer without stirring for 5 minutes until syrupy. Remove from the heat and stir in the Kirsch. When the savarin is cooked, turn it out of the tin immediately, and place it the right way up on a wire tray placed over a tray. Prick all over the savarin with a fine skewer, then slowly spoon over the hot sugar syrup. Continue spooning the syrup over the savarin until the cake becomes saturated, using the syrup that drips into the tray underneath. Leave to cool.

To serve, peel the bananas and slice thinly. Toss them immediately in the sugar syrup which has collected in the tray together with the strawberries and raspberries. Place the savarin on a serving plate, spoon the fruit into the centre and serve immediately.
Serves 6

Tarte aux pruneaux
Prune flan with pastry cream

Metric	Imperial
175 g plain flour	6 oz plain flour
pinch of salt	pinch of salt
100 g butter, chilled	4 oz butter, chilled
40 g ground almonds	1½ oz ground almonds
2 × 15 ml spoons caster sugar	2 tablespoons caster sugar
1 egg yolk	1 egg yolk
1 × 5 ml spoon water	1 teaspoon water
350 g prunes*	12 oz prunes*
150 ml dry white wine	¼ pint dry white wine
6 × 15 ml spoons redcurrant jelly	6 tablespoons redcurrant jelly
juice of ½ lemon	juice of ½ lemon

Crème pâtissière:	Crème pâtissière:
2 × 15 ml spoons cornflour	2 tablespoons cornflour
2 eggs	2 eggs
2 egg yolks	2 egg yolks
50 g caster sugar	2 oz caster sugar
450 ml milk	¾ pint milk
15 g butter	½ oz butter

Preparation time: about 1 hour, plus chilling
Cooking time: about 1 hour
Oven: 190°C, 375°F, Gas Mark 5

* Buy prunes that need no soaking before cooking – they are available in packets from most supermarkets. Other fruits can be used instead of prunes but if using pale-coloured fruits substitute sieved apricot jam for the redcurrant jelly. Do not use the glaze more than 2 hours before serving or it will seep into the custard.

Sift the flour and salt into a bowl. Cut the butter into the flour in small pieces, then rub in lightly with the fingertips. Stir in the almonds and sugar. Mix the egg yolk and water together, then stir into the flour mixture with a round-bladed knife until the mixture draws together. Form into a smooth ball with one hand, then cover and chill for 30 minutes.
Meanwhile put the prunes in a large heavy-based pan with the wine. Simmer very gently for 20–30 minutes until the prunes are plump and tender and have absorbed most of the wine. Shake the pan occasionally to stop the prunes sticking to the bottom. Remove the prunes with a slotted spoon and set aside to cool. Reserve any liquid in the pan.
Roll out the dough on a floured surface and use to line a loose-bottomed fluted 24 cm/9½ inch flan tin or flan ring set on a baking sheet. Prick the base of the dough in several places with a fork, then line with foil or greaseproof paper and fill with baking beans.
Bake the pastry 'blind' in a preheated oven for 10 minutes, then remove the paper and beans, and bake for a further 8–10 minutes until the pastry is set and lightly golden. (Take care the pastry does not burn; the addition of sugar and almonds makes it susceptible to scorching.) Set aside to cool.
Meanwhile, make the crème pâtissière. Put the cornflour in a bowl and gradually beat in the eggs, egg yolks and sugar. Beat with a wire balloon whisk or rotary beater until thick and frothy. Heat the milk to just below boiling point, then gradually beat into the egg mixture. Return the mixture to the rinsed-out pan and gradually bring to the boil, whisking constantly and vigorously with a balloon whisk until thick and smooth. Simmer for 2–3 minutes, whisking, then leave to cool for a few minutes.
Remove the flan tin or ring carefully from the pastry case and place the case on a serving plate. Pour in the crème pâtissière and dot with flecks of butter to prevent a skin forming. Allow to cool. Slit the prunes carefully along one side, then ease out the stones. Arrange the prunes in a circular pattern on top of the crème pâtissière. Put the redcurrant jelly and lemon juice into the pan containing the liquid reserved from the prunes, heat gently until the jelly has melted, then simmer for a few minutes until thickened, stirring constantly with a wooden spoon. Strain, then brush evenly over the prunes. Leave to cool before serving.
Serves 6–8

INDEX